Mechanics of the Doomsday and Life After Death

MECHANICS OF THE DOOMSDAY AND LIFE AFTER DEATH

THE ULTIMATE FATE OF THE UNIVERSE AS SEEN THROUGH THE HOLY QUR'AN

S. BASHIR UD-DIN MAHMOOD

KITAB BHAVAN
New Delhi-110002

Mechanics of the Doomsday & Life After Death

KITAB BHAVAN
Publishers, Distributors, Exporters & Importers
1784, Kalan Mahal, Darya Ganj,
New Delhi - 1100 02 (India)

Phone : (91-11) 23277392, 23274686,
: (91-11) 23263383
Mob : +91-9953098606

Website : www.kitabbhavan.net
Email : info@kitabbhavan.net
nasri@vsnl.com

Reprint : 2022

ISBN - 10 : 81-7251-133-3
ISBN - 13 : 978-81-7151-133-3

Book Code No. : M000155

Batch ID : SLVRBRT010422

Printed & Published in India by :

Moonis Ali Nasri for Kitab Bhavan
1784, Kalan Mahal, Darya Ganj,
New Delhi - 1100 02 [India]

بِسْمِ اللّٰهِ الرَّحْمٰنِ الرَّحِيْمِ ○

تَبٰرَكَ الَّذِيْ بِيَدِهِ الْمُلْكُ ز وَهُوَ عَلٰى كُلِّ شَيْءٍ

قَدِيْرُ ۙ ﴿١﴾ الَّذِيْ خَلَقَ الْمَوْتَ وَالْحَيٰوةَ لِيَبْلُوَكُمْ اَيُّكُمْ اَحْسَنُ

عَمَلًا ؕ وَهُوَ الْعَزِيْزُ الْغَفُوْرُ ۙ ﴿٢﴾ الَّذِيْ خَلَقَ سَبْعَ سَمٰوٰتٍ طِبَاقًا ؕ

مَا تَرٰى فِيْ خَلْقِ الرَّحْمٰنِ مِنْ تَفٰوُتٍ ؕ فَارْجِعِ الْبَصَرَ ۙ هَلْ

تَرٰى مِنْ فُطُوْرٍ ﴿٣﴾ ثُمَّ ارْجِعِ الْبَصَرَ كَرَّتَيْنِ يَنْقَلِبْ اِلَيْكَ

الْبَصَرُ خَاسِئًا وَّهُوَ حَسِيْرٌ ﴿٤﴾

"BLESSED BE HE IN WHOSE HANDS IS DOMINION; AND HE IS OVER ALL THINGS;

HE WHO CREATED DEATH AND LIFE,THAT HE MAY TRY WHICH OF YOU IS BEST IN DEED:AND HE IS THE EXALTED IN MIGHT,OFT-FORGIVING;

HE WHO CREATED THE SEVEN HEAVENS ONE ABOVE ANOTHER;NO WANT OF PROPORTION WILT THOU SEE IN THE CREATION OF (GOD) MOST GRACIOUS,SO TURN THY VISION AGAIN; SEEST THOU ANY FLAW?

AGAIN TURN THY VISION,A SECOND TIME:(THE) VISION WILL COME BACK TO THEE DULL AND DISCOMFITED,IN A STATE WORN OUT".

67(1-4)

PREFACE

Doomsday referred in the Holy Quran as Quaimat (قيامت), Saet (الساعة), Yom (اليوم), is an essential part of the belief of every muslim. There are hundreds of verses in the Holy Quran which describe the various events of this great happening. Muslims, in general believe in them without raising any question. However the current age of science and technology is the age of 'Doubt' also. We cannot stop people from asking, what is it? and how will it happen?

For example, Holy Quran tells us that during the period of Doomsday, oceans will boil and catch fire 81(6), 82(3,4); crust of earth will be overturned 99(1-2); atmosphere will be filled with smoke 44(10-11); mountains will fly 27(88); moon will join the sun 75(8-9); sun and the stars will be overthrown 81(1-4); universe will pulsate back to its original point of creation 21(104), heavens and earth will be recreated in different forms 14(48); there will be Resurrection and the Day of Judgement etc. etc. All that is true and we do believe it to be so. But is there any logical explanation of such happenings?

Unfortunately there is hardly any book or paper available on the subject which could answer such questions in the scientific terms, to appeal to the youth, trained to think rationally. I have been motivated by such forward looking bright muslim young men and women in the writing of this book. It is principally to satisfy their quest for the unknown.

Another reason, though of lesser importance to motivate me in writing this book has been the worldwide scientific interest in knowing about the end of the universe. A great deal of research work is now going on about the death of stars, solar systems, galaxies, and the universe. Hundreds of excellent research papers have appeared in the scientific journals on these crucial issues in recent times. Noting that Holy Quran has been the first to discuss about these issues, I was impelled to invite the attention of scientific world to the Divine Revelation, to tell them that what they were looking for now, was indeed first ecohed in the deserts of Arabia over fourteen hundreds years ago, by the unlettered prophet of Allah, may peace be upon him.

Not only that, he also made clear the Divine purpose behind the creation and the end of universe. After all science finds nothing illogical in nature, then why the Doomsday?

While attempting the solution of such fundamental questions. I have discssed in this book the sensitive subjects of human soul and life; and matters related to the life-after-death also which though currently fall out of the scope of physics,but are definitely of great importance to meta-physics.The book is thus an attempt to systematically study the complex realities of life, life-after-death and Doomsday, the ultimate fate of ourselves and of our universe, in the light of the Holy Quran and the latest scientific thought, pointing out new horizons for science; and developing a better understanding of the Future, for the believers and the non-believers alike. However, there remain too many unknowns, waiting for exploration by more and more research workers. Therefore derivations in this book should be taken as the author's view point only. May God forgive him where he has erred or failed to explain the Divine Message correctly. (Amen).

Dated 1.7.1987 S.BASHIRUDDIN MAHMOOD
Islamabad (Pakistan).

DEDICATION

AND

ACKNOWLEDGEMENT

In the name of Allah, The Beneficent, the Merciful; I dedicate this work to the best of mankind, the last of the Prophets of Allah, Muhammad (peace be upon him), on whom was completed the religion of all of the previous prophets; and Holy Quran was revealed on him through the angel Gibraeel for the guidance of all mankind. In his name I dedicate this work to the muslim youth, the proud beholder of his heritage and to my father, the Late Ch. Muhammad Sharif Khan and my mother who taught me to believe in Allah and His Messenger; and to my wife Nasim Kaifi Mahmood for her encouragement in my moments of despair while writing this book; and lastly to my sons Asim,Ahmad and Shahzad, with the prayer that may Allah lead them to the right path and accept them for Himself.

My thanks are due to the various friends and to the founder members of the Holy Quran Research Foundation, especially to Mr. Farhat Ullah Babar, Managing Director Daily Frontier Post, Ch. Fazal-e-Haq, Retd. Home Secretary, Government of Pakistan, Maj.Gen.(Retd). Abdur Rehman, Member, Government Services Tribunal, Prof. Dr. M.Iqbal, Professor of Surgeory, Dr. M. Akram Sheikh, Managing Director Pakistan Steels, Ch. Zafarullah Khan, SE, PAEC, Dr. M.M. Qurashi, Member Science Foundation, Mr. Zahid Aziz, General Manager, National Fertilizer Corporation, Mr. Ilyas Miraj, Managing Director, Ittefaque Engineering Works, Lahore and Mr. Salim Mehmud, Chairman, SUPARCO, for their constant encouragement and valuable advice during the preparation of this work. I am also greatly indebted to Mr. Hamid Majeed and to Mr. Salman Masood for their help in the editing of this work. May Allah bless them all !

Translation of the verses of the Holy Quran has been generally taken from Allama Abdullah Yousaf Ali[42], Muhammad Marmaduke Pickthal[39], and Muhammad Asad[15], may Allah reward them all for their services to Islam.

DEDICATION

AND

ACKNOWLEDGEMENT

In the name of Allah, The Beneficent the Merciful, I dedicate this work to the best of mankind, the last of the Prophets of Allah, Muhammad (peace be upon him), on whom was completed the religion of all of the previous prophets and Holy Quran was revealed on him through the angel Gibraeel for the guidance of all mankind. In his name I dedicate this work to the Muslim youth the proud beholder of his heritage and to my father, the Late Ch. Muhammad Sharif Khan and my mother who taught me to believe in Allah and His Messenger, and to my wife Nasim Fatima Mahmood for her encouragement in my moments of despair while writing this book and lastly to my sons Asim Ahmad and Shahzad, with the prayer that may Allah lead them to the right path and accept them for Himself.

My thanks are due to the various friends and to the founder members of the Holy Quran Research Foundation, especially to Mr. Farhat Ullah Babar, Managing Director Daily Frontier Post, Ch. Fazal-e-Haq, Retd. Home Secretary, Government of Pakistan, [illegible] (Retd), Abdur Rehman, Member Government Services Tribunal, Prof. Dr. [illegible], Professor of Surgery, Mr. M. Akram Sheikh, Managing Director Pakistan Steels, Ch. Zafarullah Khan, [illegible] PARC, Dr. M. M. Qureshi, Member Science Foundation, Mr. Zakir [illegible], General Manager, National Fertilizer Corporation, [illegible] Managing Director, [illegible] Engineering Works Lahore and Mr. [illegible] Mahmud, Chairman, SBP [illegible] for their constant encouragement and valuable advice during the preparation of this work. I am also greatly indebted to Mr. Hamid Masood and to Mr. Salman Masood for their help in the [illegible] of this work. May Allah bless them all!

Translation of the verses of the Holy Quran has been generally taken from Allama Abdullah Yusuf Ali, Muhammad Marmaduke Pickthall and [illegible] reward them all for their services to Islam.

FOREWORD
and
REVIEW

The Holy Quran is basically and primarily "Al-Huda" or the guidance for mankind. It guides the individual human person to behave morally and spiritually in this world so as to achieve salvation in the life hereafter. As such, though replete with scientific references, it is neither a book of strict scientific knowledge nor of mere philosophical ideas with no practical importance. The Holy Book's guiding programme is two-fold: on the ideational level it imparts to man the conscious realization of true metaphysical realities constituting "Iman" for which no single equivalent in English Language is available. Far from being dogmatic or irrational, these metaphysical truths are apprehended and endorsed by the human intellect. On the operational level, it activates the moral sense inherent in human nature for its full fruition individually and collectively.

The Quranic references to physical and cosmic phenomena serve to support its typical theistic argument. It refers to the physical phenomena as the "signs" (ayat) of His Omnipotence, All-Embracing Knowledge and Total Wisdom. The gigantic creation, the universe, with all its uniformities of causal processes, is a prime "sign" (ayat) or proof of its Maker. In addition to cosmogony, these Quranic rereferences mostly relate to physics, astronomy, geology, embryology and psychology, etc. The correct meaning of these references could not be understood by early exegetical writers because the amount of scientific knowledge was extremely limited at that time. But now, as the vista of human knowledge in various branches of physical sciences has expanded enormously, we can have better appreciation of these allusions.

The process of re-focussing the attention of Muslims on the Quran started with Shah Waliullah of Delhi in the eighteenth century of Christian era. After passing through many stages during the ninteenth century it seems to be nearing its zenith in the present time. Allama Iqbal's "Reconstruction of Religious Thought in Islam" is an important landmark in this field and he definitely added a new dimension to this process by endeavouring to assert and affirm the Islamic faith on the basis of higher physics and higher psychology. Dr. Mohammad Rafiuddin carried his work forward especially in the realm of psychological theories in his "Ideology of the Future". More recently, the eminent French Surgeon, Maurice Bucaille has reasserted the veracity of Quranic references to biological phenomena, in particular, embrylogy. In addition to that many authors have taken up the task of explaining Quranic References relating to the fields of Physics and Astronomy on the basis of recent research and discoveries. Indeed, as yet no scientific observation or theory has contravened any of the Quranic descriptions of physical phenomena. This by itself is an ample proof of the claim made by the Holy Book in Ayah 53 of Surah 41:

> Soon will We show them our signs
> in the cosmos and within their
> own selves, until it becomes
> manifest to them that this is the truth.

The belief in the ultimate end of man's earthly existence (al-akhira) is central to the whole system of the Quranic teachings on eschatology. The basic idea here is that there will come a moment, "The Hour" (Al-sa'a) when every human being will be shaken into a unique and unprecedented selfawareness of his deeds. "When the great cataclysm comes, that day man will recall what he had been striving for" (79:34-35) is a typical statement of this great episode. Mr. S. Bashir-ud-Din, the author of this book, has very ably put together the events which will, according to the Quran, lead to the Doomsday—the Day of final reckoning. What is commendable in his exposition of this theme is that he has presented it in the light of modern scientific theories and speculation, thus showing mostly the corroboration of divine revelation with scientific thought. In a book of this nature it is difficult to agree with the author on all minor points of detail and interpretation; but I do favourably appreciate the general plan and purpose of the book. May Allah (SWT) reward him for this noble task. I also congratulate him on the formation of Holy Quran Research Foundation in Islamabad. Living in a scientific ethos, we surely need more studies and publications in this vein to enkindle and rejuvenate genuine religious faith in the sceptical minds of our age. May Allah help members of the Foundation's Governing Body in their future projects.

DR. ISRAR AHMAD
Founder-President
Markazi Anjuman Khuddamul Quran Lahore
36–K Model Town Lahore (Pakistan).

Markazi Anjuman Khuddamul Quran Lahore

Mr. Bashiruddin Mahmood's book on "Doomsday and Life after Death " comes at a very significant time. It's appearance coincides with a dangerous intellectual crisis in the Elite of the Islamic world. This Elite is overawed by the western Progress in Scientific Knowledge and exploitation of matter, and universe. To add to the Tragedy it is this agitated and frustrated elite, including our youth that exercises or is likely in near future to assume intellectual and cultural leadership of muslim Communities. Then, there is the other, the Conservative Elite who are currently the Custodians of power in the Ummah and generally live and think in the past inspite of their claim to be the heralders of a so-called Islamic Resurgence. I feel that Mr. Mahmood's book is specially addressed to these two classes on whose intellectual reclamation, our future apparently hinges. Their double-standard, and bi-directional Sojourn on the ship of time is heart-rending. Their travel reminds one of the anguish and torment that Late Dr. Iqbal once experienced in a travel from Europe to Lahore. His ship passed by the Coast of Sicily in a Star-lit night. The moment-a whole night we are told-transported the Poet of the East to distant past. Shaken to the Soul, he said.

رو لے اب جی بھر کے اے دیدۂ خوننابہ بار
وہ نظر آتا ہے تہذیب حجازی کا مزار

The present State of intellectual horizon of the Muslim Elite is no less soul-shaking than the star-lit Sicilian Coast encountered by Dr. Iqbal. Reclamation of this almost lost and always wavering muslim intellect of today is possible. If we fail in that reclamation they may, in heritage leave only a heart-rending Sicily. This reclamation will not be achieved through SEMINARS, WORKSHOPS, and Discussion Forums inspired and organized on

Harvard and Washington pattern. It will be achieved through a fresh, time-oriented and Science-based interpretation of Quran which is the bed-rock of our existence and the flag for our forward march

Can Sciences like Physics, and Astrophysics be employed to reveal the mysteries of Doomsday and of dead matter returning to life , of Resurrection and of Day of judgement for the benefit of the Muslims caught between the time-honoured Conventionalism and breath-taking revelations of Science about time, space, and universe? Will the un-impeachable sanctity of Quran permit this? yes. All this and more is possible. Mr. Mahmood's book demonstrates that ——patient research will bring out hidden treasures of knowledge about univers; its creation; its transformation through the instruments of its Galaxies Stars, and planets, and inter-alia the methods and Mechanics that God employs and is constantly employing to lead our earth to its Doomsday; the mankind to their Day of Reckoning; and the universe to rebirth. The book demonstrates beyond doubt that Frontiers of knowledge conquered by Modern Physics and Astrophysics in twentieth century were clearly identified by the Divine revelation and His Prophet (S.A.S), fifteen centuries ago. In that context, the book is a stern reminder to the Administrations and Governments of all Muslim States that their efforts in interpreting and disseminating the last message of Allah have been highly inadequate. It reminds them that the star-lit sea of Science, Philosophy, wisdom, and knowledge contained in Quran is awaiting their attention. They must wake up if they don't wish to disappear from the contest for Political and Moral ascendence in the Globe. The book revealed to a Prophet (SAS), who called himself the "City of knowledge" انا مدينة العلم ,and is for all mankind for all the times.

The author has, with astonishing clarity and success, shown how known inter-stellar, and inter-Galactic events in time and space can destroy this earth and universe leading to emergence of a new universe accompanied by a day of reckoning for all intelligent beings. He has marvellous ability of narrating advanced theories of modern spatial Sciences in entirely non-technical and everyday language, and relating them to relevant Quranic Verses. While proceeding with the book, the reader feels as if the entire fundamental knowledge of Modern Physics and principles of Creation and Recreation of Cosmic Carvan assembled by the western Scientists were borrowed from Quran. Very elaborate but simple charts and graphs have been added to facilitate the un-initiated reader to grasp technical Scientific theories and processes without any difficulty.

The work is an unprecedented and inspiring adventure in a field heretofore left un-explored by Muslim writers. Even the western Scholars of Comparative study of Science and religion have not yet dealt with the subjects of Doomsday; day of judgement; and Resurrection although these are TOPICS common to Bible and Quran. The reading public will, I am sure thank the author for introducing them to such new horizons of thought and literature. May God grant him and his Foundation greater courage and ability to expand this activity of research and interpretation of Quran in the language of Science. AMEN.

Islamabad. Ch. Fazl-e-Haq,
August, 1987. (Retd) Home Secretary,
Government of Pakistan.

The book "Mechanics of the Doomsday and Life after Death" is a singular contribution to Quran and Science series by S.Bashiruddin Mahmood. The author has been genuinely inspired to extend his scientific thought into metaphysics — a realm which again highlights tremendous challenges that lie ahead. Metaphysics does not lend itself to simple scientific parameters of this twentieth century. The instances of soul and its development, the assertion that only human kind has been blessed with soul, consciousness of electron & biochemical basis for definition of life, the unpredictability of time-frame for Doomsday/Day of Judgement with obvious estimates varying from a few hundred to millions of years the "momentum" phase of soul after earthly life (Burzakh), parallel pattern between spiritual causes and physical causes triggering events in time - space, "The other Worlds" and nature of life there, etc. etc. open new horizons of thought for further thought and work.

I cannot resist an inner urge to sound a note of caution for scientists, scientific scholars as well as theologists of Islam. The orthodox religious scholars certainly need to sharpen and widen their visions to keep pace with dynamism of Islam, and should not be shy of exploding scientific knowledge and modern achievements. By the same token, the Muslim Scientists and intellectuals would not find religious dimensions amenable to scientific method essentially limited in scope. Even pure logic won't fathom the Islamic metaphysics. Thus scientists and intellectuals should not display overenthusiasm by questionable interpretations of Holy Quran just to establish that each and every scientific theory is either revealed in the Holy Book or provides confirmation to scientific hypotheses. Till Doomsday and hereafter, the men of science would propose, modify and reject their scientific theories but Eternal Message of Allah (J.J.) would continue to serve as beacon light for ever!

The author and Holy Quran Research Foundation (HQR) is sincerely congratulated for this extremely inspiring contribution especially during the close of epoch making 20th century A.D./ 15th century Hijra. This book answers many questions in scientific terms, appeals to the rational minds, opens new vistas into unknowns and offers many workable hypotheses for future. May Allah bless the author and his compatriots. Amin!

Islamabad.
August, 1987.

C.M.Anwar Khan, Ph.D.
20-Gosha-i-Anwar,
St.13, F-8/3, Islamabad.

The Quran — the Words of Allah, revealed to the Holy Prophet, fourteen cent. ago, per se, is not a book of science and yet it has about 750 Ayats which deal with scientific phenomenon in one way or the other. While some of these Ayats are easily comprehensible, the contents of the others are still beyond our grasp. As the scientific knowledge builds up with rapid advancement in various fields, the wealth of knowledge contained in the Quran is dawning upon us.

It is a very encouraging sign that of late renewed vigour is being shown by the Islamic scholars to understand the Quran in its multi-faceted dimensions. The book "Mechanics of the Doomsday and Life after Death" authored by Mr. S.Bashiruddin Mahmood is a bold attempt in that direction. It is the outcome of his painstaking research study extending over several years. The most important aspect of the book is that it is an analysis of selected Ayats by an engineer who has deep understanding of Islam as well as a good grasp of engineering and sciences especially Astronomy. The author has chosen some very apt and powerful Ayats to give their interpretation in various chapters of the book in a simple and direct manner to develop the main theme of his book. The analysis has been strengthened with the help of similies and interesting diagrams and pictures. The fact is that this work is so absorbing that the reader proceeds with increasing interest from beginning to the end of the book — once started one does not like to stop before finishing it.

I am confident that this work will serve to encourage scholars of all thoughts to embark upon in-depth analysis of the Quran from various aspects falling in their fields of specialization with the intent to acquire fuller understanding of the Quran. Each pause, word, verse and Ayet calls for careful attention, thinking and reflection and this is where the men and women with vision can come in very handy for the true understanding of the teachings of the glorious Quran, wherein lies the salvation not only of the mankind but also of what constitutes the universe as a whole.

Karachi,
August, 1987.

Salim Mehmud,
Chairman,
Pakistan Space & Upper Atmosphere Research Commission,
Karachi.

CONTENTS

Part—I.

Nature of the Doomsday and the ultimate End of the universe.

Chapter — I.

INTRODUCTION

"And Unto Allah belongs,
The Unseen of the heavens
and the earth,
And the matter of the Hour
(of Doom) is,
But as the twinkling of the eye,
Or it is nearer still,
Lo, Allah is able to do all things"
....16(77)

﴿٧٧﴾ وَلِلَّهِ غَيْبُ ٱلسَّمَٰوَٰتِ وَٱلْأَرْضِ ۚ وَمَآ
أَمْرُ ٱلسَّاعَةِ إِلَّا كَلَمْحِ ٱلْبَصَرِ أَوْ هُوَ أَقْرَبُ ۚ
إِنَّ ٱللَّهَ عَلَىٰ كُلِّ شَىْءٍ قَدِيرٌ

All the religions of the world and also the modern science, believes that the world is going to end, but the question remains, how? When we look around at the vast skies studded with stars, we do ask ourselves, what will eventually happen to all this? In our hearts we are also concerned about our own existence. Will this beautiful world of ours, also perish? Though these are serious questions, yet, unfortunately our knowledge about them is next to nothing. This book is an effort to probe into the unknown, with the hope to atleast partially satisfy the curiosity to know about the ultimate fate of the universe. Our thesis is based upon our understanding of the Holy Quran, the Divine revelation available before us in the purest form; and the current scientific developmentson this subject.

In the olden times, Greeks had advanced the hypothesis of eternity of universe, saying that it had always existed. This notion persists among a number of leading astronomers even now who believe in the continuity of the universe. According to this theory [1,18] matter creates more matter and the cosmos goes on expanding for ever.

However, this view has been rejected by an equally large number of scientists. Based upon their observations of the formation of galaxies, expansion of the universe, decay of matter and study of the behavior of the elementary particles, they believe in a finite universe, both in terms of space and time. In this regard the currently popular scientific views were summed up in Geneva, in a conference of cosmologists and particle physicists held in November 1983, by the renowned physicist Stephen Hawking of Cambridge.[2] He said; "What we look back on as the 'Big Bang', was a time of very high but not infinite density, a state to which universe will precisely return through collapse after its present expansion phase is over. Out of the high density phase, it will be born again (with an exponential inflation phase), to repeat the cycle and infinitium".

As to the religions, according to Paul Davies,[10] they differ greatly in their conception of the moment and manner of the cosmic demise. Some warn of imminent catastrophe of a world overtaken by apocalyptic destruction when the sinful will be judged sternly. Others teach about a forthcoming Kingdom of Heaven which will replace the harsh and uncertain world we live in. Some Oriental religions incline towards a cyclical system where the end of this world precedes the rebirth of another.

On this subject guidance received from the Holy Quran is most comprehensive and unparallel in clarity. Fundamentally it says that this universe is a finite universe, in which everything is made with a purpose, at the fulfilment of which it will perish according to some pre-fixed measurement of God,

٣-مَا خَلَقْنَا السَّمٰوٰتِ وَالْاَرْضَ وَمَا بَيْنَهُمَآ
اِلَّا بِالْحَقِّ وَاَجَلٍ مُّسَمًّى

"We have not created the
heavens and the earth,
And all that lies between them,
but with a purpose,
According to a pre-fixed measurement.
. . . . . .46(3).

Thus every thing in the universe follows a time table. After their purpose of existence is fulfilled, they are replaced by the better suited ones for the new demands. Ultimate scenario is given by the following verse:—

﴿٢٦﴾ كُلُّ مَنْ عَلَيْهَا فَانٍ
﴿٢٧﴾ وَّيَبْقٰى وَجْهُ رَبِّكَ
ذُو الْجَلٰلِ وَالْاِكْرَامِ

All that is there (in the universe),
Will perish,
Except the Face of thy Lord,
Full of Majesty, Bounty and Honour"
. . . . 55(26-27)

From these verses we can derive that nothing is everlasting. Everything that has a beginning must have its end. When its time comes it will not be postponed 71(4). On this principle we can say that even very stable particles such as neutrons and protons cannot have infinite life but will decay with time. In the final analysis whole of the universe would be annihilated. Everlasting Reality is that of God only.

This is the principle of "Finiteness" which follows the Divine scheme of pre-programmed events about which Holy Quran says;

"Every order (event) has an
appointed time,
And ye will come to know"
. . . .6(67).

لِّكُلِّ نَبَإٍ مُّسْتَقَرٌّ وَسَوْفَ تَعْلَمُونَ ٦٧

This also means that nature is logical in its design and events unfold themselves following a pre-set destiny called Taqdeer (تقدير) in the Holy Quran which is the in-built Divine measurement and design life of things, and guides things to their natural ends. On this the Quran says:—

"Glorify the Name of your
Lord, Most high,
Who creates and proportions,
Who measures then guides"
. . . 87(1-3).

١ سَبِّحِ اسْمَ رَبِّكَ الْأَعْلَى
٢ الَّذِي خَلَقَ فَسَوَّىٰ
٣ وَالَّذِي قَدَّرَ فَهَدَىٰ

"Our Lord is He,
Who gave everything its nature,
and directs it (through life)"
. . . 20(50)

٥٠ قَالَ رَبُّنَا الَّذِي أَعْطَىٰ كُلَّ شَيْءٍ
خَلْقَهُ ثُمَّ هَدَىٰ

And of all things
Have We taken account
In a clear Book
(of evidence)
. . . .36(12)

وَكُلَّ شَيْءٍ أَحْصَيْنَاهُ
فِي إِمَامٍ مُّبِينٍ

From these basic principles one can say nothing is there haphazard or illogical because it is against the very nature of the Creator. Thus if one can understand laws of God and analyse the effect of all the variables involved therein, then every event must be predictable. However, since our reach in time and space is limited and universe is so vast and complex, mankind may never know, with certainity, of anything, what to say of the Doomsday, the ultimate fate of universe. Sure guidance can only be through the revelation from the Creator of the worlds Himself.

Holy Quran is that very guidance, preserved for us in its purest form exactly as it was delivered by the Prophet of Allah fourteen hundred years ago to his immediate followers. Though primarily concerned with the moral reformation of mankind, yet in its many verses, it has described the events concerning the end of the present order of existence in precise and simple manner, which when co-related can give us a comprehensive view of the scenario of the end of our world and that of the whole of the universe also. The book in hand is an effort toward this direction. In it we shall see that events related to the ultimate fate of universe or Doomsday, are actually the culmination of various localized minor events which keep occuring always in the cosmos. Accordingly, even at this very moment, somewhere in space, there is some star or planet which is there now, but would not be there in the moments to follow. The day may not be too far off, when our earth and solar system will also meet its doomsday. For us, no doubt it would be a big event but for other worlds, it may pass unnoticed in the vastness of universe. Finally there would come the Day of the 'Ultimate Fate' the Final End of the entire order of present existence. But that End is also not for ever. It would give birth to a New Order of Existence, which will then remain for ever; a Future built on the shadows of the Past, a world as a consequence of the present world; a place of refinement, reward and punishment for all those who had been ever there in the frame work of time and space. In this framework, human personality or mind manifested by its soul, keeps striving on the path traced by it during its worldly existence. There it will have the consciousness but not the choice to change its course. In the overall framework of time and space Fig.I shows the various phases of our existence.

Fig. 1:

Three stages of the existence highlighted at the very opening of the Holy Quran.

Scenario of the universe is spread over three phases, history of which we find squeezed in the very opening of the Holy Quran; A represen tation of this is depicted in the following figure. Here the phase one is the pre universe, phase synomous with the characteristic Rab (رب) of the Creator which means, the one Who prearrange all means of sustenance for the events to follow. Thus He created pre universe, out of which He created the present universe which is a visible manifestation of His compassion and Beauty which we see all around. This will be followed by the 3rd and final phase of existence, that is the phase of accountability, which is connected with the Quranic concept of Doomsday, the phase when everything will return to Allah 53(42):–

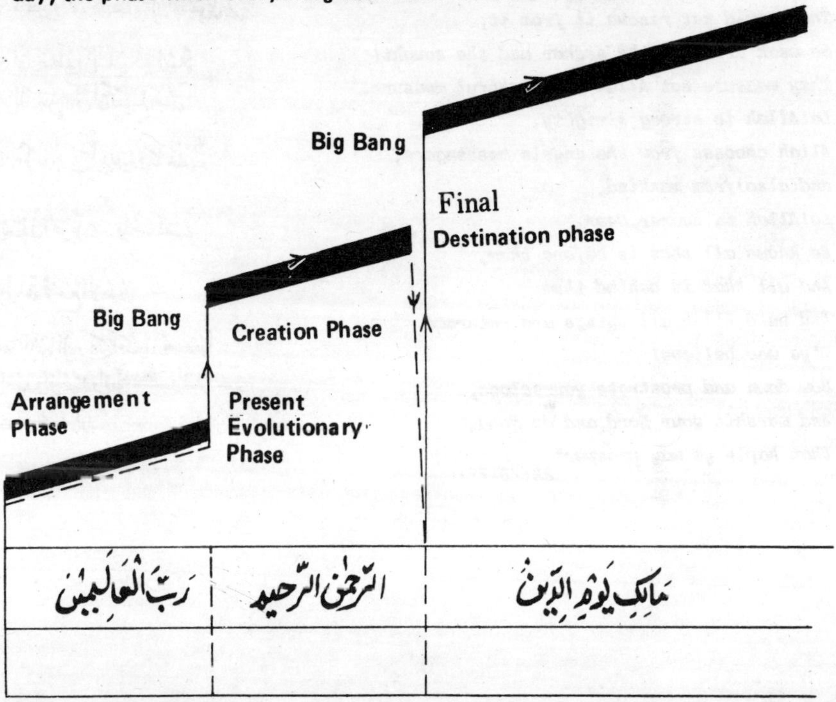

And cry not unto any other god along with Allah,
There is no God save Him,
Everything will perish save His Countanence
His is the command,
and unto Him ye will be brought back.
. . . .28(88)

وَلَا تَدْعُ مَعَ اللَّهِ إِلَٰهًا آخَرَ لَا إِلَٰهَ إِلَّا هُوَ كُلُّ شَيْءٍ هَالِكٌ إِلَّا وَجْهَهُ لَهُ الْحُكْمُ وَإِلَيْهِ تُرْجَعُونَ ﴿٨٨﴾

O Mankind!
A similitude is coined,
So pay ye heed to it.
Lo!those on whom you call beside Allah,
will never create(even)a fly
Though they combine together for the purpose.
And if the fly took something from them,
They could not rescue it from it,
So weak are(both)the seeker and the sought!
They measure not Allah His rightful measure.
Lo!Allah is strong,Almighty.
Allah chooses from the angels messengers,
and(also)from mankind,
Lo!Allah is Hearer,Seer.
He knows all that is before them,
And all that is behind them
And unto Allah all things are returned
O'ye who believe!
Bow down and prostrate yourselves,
And worship your Lord,and do good,
that haply ye may prosper"
22(73-77)

٧٣ يَا أَيُّهَا النَّاسُ ضُرِبَ مَثَلٌ فَاسْتَمِعُوا لَهُ
إِنَّ الَّذِينَ تَدْعُونَ مِنْ دُونِ اللَّهِ لَنْ يَخْلُقُوا ذُبَابًا
وَلَوِ اجْتَمَعُوا لَهُ وَإِنْ يَسْلُبْهُمُ الذُّبَابُ شَيْئًا
لَا يَسْتَنْقِذُوهُ مِنْهُ ضَعُفَ الطَّالِبُ
وَالْمَطْلُوبُ
٧٤ مَا قَدَرُوا اللَّهَ حَقَّ قَدْرِهِ إِنَّ اللَّهَ لَقَوِيٌّ عَزِيزٌ
٧٥ اللَّهُ يَصْطَفِي مِنَ الْمَلَائِكَةِ رُسُلًا
وَمِنَ النَّاسِ إِنَّ اللَّهَ سَمِيعٌ بَصِيرٌ
٧٦ يَعْلَمُ مَا بَيْنَ أَيْدِيهِمْ وَمَا خَلْفَهُمْ
بِالْعَدْلِ وَهُوَ عَلَىٰ صِرَاطٍ مُسْتَقِيمٍ
وَإِلَى اللَّهِ تُرْجَعُ الْأُمُورُ
٧٧ يَا أَيُّهَا الَّذِينَ آمَنُوا ارْكَعُوا
وَاسْجُدُوا وَاعْبُدُوا رَبَّكُمْ وَافْعَلُوا الْخَيْرَ
لَعَلَّكُمْ تُفْلِحُونَ

Chapter--2

NATURE OF THE DOOMSDAY

"It is Allah Who creates and recreates,
From the very beginning"
....85(13)

﴿١٣﴾ إِنَّهُۥ هُوَ يُبۡدِئُ وَيُعِيدُ

This verse gives a dynamic picture of the universe in which process of recreation and recreation is ever going on and on everywhere. Sometimes there also occur major shakeups or revolutionary changes in nature. Doomsdays represent such changes. From the Holy Quran we see Four types of such Doomsday.

i. Minor events of routine nature.
ii. Major events.
iii. The ultimate event of the Universal Scale.
iv. Resurrection.

In the following is given a brief review of these events which will be latter discussed in detail in the subsequent chapters. Fig—2 shows a sequential occurance of these events.

(i) Minor Events

Minor events are of routine nature, part of the continuous Divine process of creation and recreation. They represent step changes in the evolution of the world. In their scope, they may even be limited to a particular region of an earth only. On some what larger scale they effect the individual worlds, solar systems, and galaxies. However, always, they are the localized affairs limited to a particular regiononly. Depending upon their severity, they can be classified in the following types:

(a) Sub Events: These represent catasrophies on national or global scale which sometimesfall on our world, but life continues normally after they have passed over. Examples are Flood of Nooh, Ice ages, catastrophic fall of meteors etc. Holy Quran refers to such events at various places, as a reminder to reflect in the

Fig.2: Steps leadinc to the Universal Doomsday:

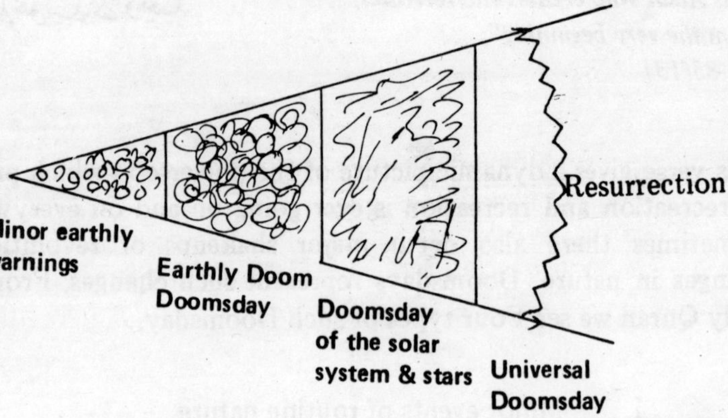

Each things has a prefixed destiny. Universe is also created for a finite period. Revelation is:

"Allah created not the heavens and the earth and all that is between them, save with truth, and for a destined end. But truly many of the mankind are disbelievers in the meeting with their Lord"...30(8).Thus heaven and earth are not for ever. This speaks of the universal Doomsday and the universal Resurrection. But before that individual worlds andearthswill have their own Doomsday at their own appointed times Not only that even individual nations have their appointed term as the Quran says: "And every nation has its term, and when its term comes they cannot put it off an hour nor yet advance it"....7(34).

Individual national Doomsday or great regional catastrophies are thus part of the story of the earthly Doomsday. Prophet of Allah warned, "when there are frequent earthquakes and red wind dust storms, wait for the earthly Doomsday". Earthly Doomsday will be followed by the large scale destruction of our galactic world. Sun and stars will be destroyed. As for other worlds this process also goes on and on in them till the end of*the universe fate of earlier generations of mankind on earth. Following verses give a typical account of one such happening which was initiated by a mighty blast in some region of our earth:

"So they were rightly seized by
a mighty blast,
And We turned them into mouldy rubbish,
A good riddance of the wicked people,
Then after them We raised other generation
No nation can live beyond the
allotted time, or lag behind, - - - - - - - -
So We made one follow the other
(to its doom)
And turned them into by-gone tales" - - -
. . . 23(41-44)

٤١ فَأَخَذَتْهُمُ الصَّيْحَةُ بِالْحَقِّ فَجَعَلْنَاهُمْ غُثَاءً
فَبُعْدًا لِلْقَوْمِ الظَّالِمِينَ
٤٢ ثُمَّ أَنشَأْنَا مِن بَعْدِهِمْ قُرُونًا آخَرِينَ
٤٣ مَا تَسْبِقُ مِنْ أُمَّةٍ أَجَلَهَا وَمَا يَسْتَأْخِرُونَ
٤٤ ثُمَّ أَرْسَلْنَا رُسُلَنَا تَتْرَا كُلَّ مَا جَاءَ أُمَّةً
رَسُولُهَا كَذَّبُوهُ فَأَتْبَعْنَا بَعْضَهُم بَعْضًا
وَجَعَلْنَاهُمْ أَحَادِيثَ فَبُعْدًا لِقَوْمٍ لَا يُؤْمِنُونَ

History of earth is witness to many such doomsdays, which fell upon individual nations and they were wiped out suddenly. Reasons of their occurance are described in Chapter—3

(b) Earthly Doomsday: This is relatively a major catastrophy which will destroy our earth with every thing in it. For us it would be a scene of ultimate destruction but on the universal scale it will be of little significance. A glimpse of this event is visible from the following verses: Detailed discussion of the subject will be found in the chapters 7 to 13.

"Further, they ask,
when will this promise (come to pass),
If what ye say (about the Doomsday)
is true?"
They will not want for aught,
But a single Blast,
It will seize them while,
They are disputing among themselves
Then, no chance will they have, by will
To dispose (of their affairs), nor,
To return to their own people"
. . . .36(48-50).

٤٨ وَيَقُولُونَ مَتَىٰ هَٰذَا الْوَعْدُ إِن كُنتُمْ
صَادِقِينَ
٤٩ مَا يَنظُرُونَ إِلَّا صَيْحَةً وَاحِدَةً
تَأْخُذُهُمْ وَهُمْ يَخِصِّمُونَ
٥٠ فَلَا يَسْتَطِيعُونَ تَوْصِيَةً وَلَا إِلَىٰ أَهْلِهِمْ
يَرْجِعُونَ

Obviously these verses have spoken of the doomsday of the whole earth concerning mankind of this planet only. That will be the end of all type of life on earth. There-after all generations of earthly people will join together in the death state, to wait together for the comming of the Day of Resurrection, which would occur after the "universal Doomsday," and at which the entire mankind from everywhere in the cosmos will be gathered before the Lord.

The concept that earthly Doomsday is separate from the Universal Doomsday, is apparent from the Sura Ar-Rahman. In its verses 55(26-45), while highlighting the order of various events leading to the ultimate Doomsday, Allah warns us that the time is not too far off when turn of our earth is to come and God will bring its doomsday. The verse 55(31) says:

"Soon shall We be free for you,
O! ye twain burden of (earth)"
. . .55(31).

٣١ سَنَفۡرُغُ لَكُمۡ أَيُّهَ ٱلثَّقَلَانِ

Obviously the tone of this verse speaks about the pre-occupation of the Creator in some happening of similar nature, somewhere else in the universe at this very time.

(ii) Major Events:

These events happen on cosmological scale which involve atleast destruction of a solar system but on larger scale, may include a part, or the entire galaxy also. The following Quranic verse speaks of one such future event which will destroy our solar system and some part of our galaxy also:

"(Watch for the Day),
When the Sun is folded up,
When the stars fall,
Loosing their light"
81(1-2)

١ إِذَا ٱلشَّمۡسُ كُوِّرَتۡ

٢ وَإِذَا ٱلنُّجُومُ ٱنكَدَرَتۡ

(iii) Ultimate event of universal Doomsday:

This will happen once for all, and would involve the whole of the universe. At its climax, there will remain nothing but God alone, a state of affairs described by the following revelation of the Holy Quran:

"(Ultimately)
All that is there will perish,
Except the Face of your Lord,
Full of Majesty, Bounty and Honour"
. . . .55(26-27).

٢٦- كُلُّ مَنْ عَلَيْهَا فَانٍ ۝
٢٧- وَيَبْقَىٰ وَجْهُ رَبِّكَ
ذُو الْجَلَالِ وَالْإِكْرَامِ ۝

Thus the ultimate event means the end of the entire order of the present physical universe, reversing back to the original state of existence in the pre-universe period, when there was nothing but God alone, a state of "Nothingness".

(iv) Resurrection: (يوم الدين) This is the Last Event of the present phase of Existence. All the minor and the major doomsdays culminate into it. This will be only for once and would mark the beginning of a new universe, much more bigger and grander than the entire order of the present existence.

Day of Resurrection would also be initiated suddenly. At its prime, all people, of all the times will be brought back to life and judged according to their deeds performed in their previous lives. In the new universe there will be the Jannat (جنّت) the abode of the righteous and the Jahannam (جهنّم), the abode of the wicked. Following are some of the Quranic verses highlighting the events of the Day of Resurrection:

"The bugle(صور) shall be sounded,
when behold!
From their sepulchres,
Mankind will then rush forth to
their Lord"

٥١ وَنُفِخَ فِي الصُّورِ فَإِذَا هُمْ مِنَ الْأَجْدَاثِ إِلَىٰ
رَبِّهِمْ يَنْسِلُونَ

"They will say, Ah' Woe unto us!
Who has raised us up from
our beds of repose?
(Then they will know), This
is what (Allah)
Most Gracious had promised
And true was the word of
the apostles!

٥٢ قَالُوا يَا وَيْلَنَا مَنْ بَعَثَنَا مِنْ مَرْقَدِنَا ۜ هَٰذَا
مَا وَعَدَ الرَّحْمَٰنُ وَصَدَقَ الْمُرْسَلُونَ

Fig.3: Small scale Doomsdays of the stars, solar systems and of the planets are a routine in the universe which consists of millions of galaxies, while each galaxy may consist of trillions of heavenly bodies. Even by our best telescope we only see a part of the heavenly world. What is beyond that, no body knows. But the astronomers have seen that heavens are extremely dynamic organisms. Here thousands of the stars are dying and many more get birth at the same time. The photograph of the heaven taken with a 10 inch f/4,5 Newtonion, by the Australian Cris Floyd, shows the part of the heavenly world only. Who can say that the bright nebula at the top right corner was not once a living world which is undergoing its Doomsday now?

"It will be no more than a single Blast,
When Lo! they will be brought
before us!

٥٣ إِن كَانَتْ إِلَّا صَيْحَةً وَاحِدَةً فَإِذَا هُمْ جَمِيعٌ
لَّدَيْنَا مُحْضَرُونَ

"Then on that Day,
Not a single soul will be wronged,
in the least,
But repay the meeds of
the past deeds"
....36(51-54)

٥٤ فَالْيَوْمَ لَا تُظْلَمُ نَفْسٌ شَيْئًا وَلَا تُجْزَوْنَ إِلَّا
مَا كُنتُمْ تَعْمَلُونَ

SUMMARY OF DIFFERENT PHASES OF THE DOOMSDAY AS SEEN THROUGH THE SURA-AR-RAHMAN

Various stages in the Doomsday leading to the ultimate universal end are apparent from the verses 55(29—47) of sura Ar-Rehman, which start with the pre amble that at the end of this universe all that is in it will be destroyed, leaving the Singularity of God only. It has been revealed:—

٢٦- كُلُّ مَنْ عَلَيْهَا فَانٍ

"All that is there will perish,
Except the Face of your Lord,
Full of majesty, Bountry and Honour"
.....55(26-28)

٢٧- وَيَبْقَىٰ وَجْهُ رَبِّكَ
ذُو الْجَلَالِ وَالْإِكْرَامِ

The next verse speaks of the dynamic nature of the universe, which is full of living worlds like ours, all of which have their doomsday at their turns.

"Of Him seeks (its needs)
Every one in the heavens and the earth,
Every Day, He is in the New Splendour,
Then which of the favours,
Of your Lord will ye deny"
....55(29–30)

٢٩ يَسْأَلُهُ مَن فِي السَّمَاوَاتِ وَالْأَرْضِ كُلَّ يَوْمٍ
هُوَ فِي شَأْنٍ
٣٠ فَبِأَيِّ آلَاءِ رَبِّكُمَا تُكَذِّبَانِ

The next verse speaks of the turn of the Doomsday of our earth:

"Soon shall We be free for you,
O both ye burdens (of earth)
(That is men and women, or mankind and jinns).
Then which of the favours of your Lord,
will ye deny".
. . . . .55(31–32).

٣١ سَنَفْرُغُ لَكُمْ أَيُّهَ الثَّقَلَانِ
٣٢ فَبِأَيِّ آلَاءِ رَبِّكُمَا تُكَذِّبَانِ

In this verse, the reference "Soon We shal be free for you", speaks of the business of the Lord in the affairs of some other worlds at this time; but it is a warning to us on earth that our turn is not far off.

Before its Doomsday the inhabitant of the earth will have attained a very high degree of technological civilization. It is apparent from the following verse:—

O! Ye assembly of Jinns and Men!
If it be, ye can pass beyond
the zones of the heavens and the earth,
Try to pass them!
Not without authority or Power,
Shall ye be able to Pass!
Then which of the favours of your Lord,
will ye then deny".
. . . . .55(33–34)

٣٣ يَٰمَعْشَرَ الْجِنِّ وَالْإِنسِ إِنِ اسْتَطَعْتُمْ
أَن تَنفُذُوا مِنْ أَقْطَارِ السَّمَٰوَٰتِ
وَالْأَرْضِ فَانفُذُوا لَا تَنفُذُونَ إِلَّا بِسُلْطَٰنٍ
٣٤ فَبِأَيِّ آلَاءِ رَبِّكُمَا تُكَذِّبَانِ

It also seems from these verses that before the actual Doomsday, living conditions on earth will become unbearable. Mankind and Jinns, all will try to leave for outer space and with power they will be able to do so. However, as they do so there will be no escape for them, as we may see from the following verses;

"On you will be sent
A flame of fire (to burn)
And a smoke (to choke)
against which no defence will ye have.
Then which of the favours of your Lord will they deny"
. . . .55(35–36).

٣٥ يُرْسَلُ عَلَيْكُمَا شُوَاظٌ مِّن نَّارٍ وَنُحَاسٌ
فَلَا تَنتَصِرَانِ
٣٦ فَبِأَيِّ آلَاءِ رَبِّكُمَا تُكَذِّبَانِ

These verses refer to the perils of the space flight at the start up of the earthly Doomsdays. There will be the intense burst of radiation and hot plasma of gases. A glimpse of it we may see in the solar flares also. This will be followed by the earthly Doomsday, which will destroy it entirely.

Even after this the, Doomsdays of other earth-hke-bodies may continue. But finally there comes the universal Doomsday which will involve the entire heavens. At this time the average radiation temperature in the universe is only 3°Kelvin, but then it will rise high, giving the sky the look of a red hot molten bath of copper. This means that universe will become very hot. Science predicts such a situation when the universe begins to contract and as it reduces in size, its temperature will rise, rendering it into a hot plasma of gases. Ultimately nothing will remain, except the Singularity of the Creator only. Following verses seem to refer to the ultimate universal Doomsday:—

٣٧ فَإِذَا انشَقَّتِ السَّمَاءُ فَكَانَتْ وَرْدَةً
كَالدِّهَانِ
٣٨ فَبِأَيِّ آلَاءِ رَبِّكُمَا تُكَذِّبَانِ

When the sky is rent asunder
And it becomes red like a molten
bath of copper.
Then which of the favours of your Lord,
You may deny".
. . . 55(37-38)

Universal Doomsday will be followed by a period of re-creation of a new type of universe Sura Abraham verses 48, throws light on this happening in the following manner:—

٤٨- يَوْمَ تُبَدَّلُ الْأَرْضُ غَيْرَ الْأَرْضِ
وَالسَّمٰوٰتُ وَبَرَزُوْا لِلّٰهِ
الْوَاحِدِ الْقَهَّارِ ۝

(Look for the Day)
when the earth will be changed
to other than the Earth,
heavens also will be changed,
And they will come forth unto Allah,
The One, the Almighty.
. . . . .14(48)

Final phase is the phase of Resurrection, which will come after the universal Doomsday. At this, all mankind and the Jinns of everywhere, of all the times, will be brought back to life, and presented for their accountability. Their deeds would themselves speaks for them. This will be followed by the reward and punish-

ment phase, which will then continue for ever and ever.

"On that Day No question will be asked,
of mankind or Jinn as to his sin;
Then which of the favours of your Lord
will ye deny?
For sinner will be known by their marks,
And they will be seized by their fore locks,
and their feet,
Then which is the favours of your, ye will deny".
....55(39–40)

فَيَوْمَئِذٍ لَّا يُسْـَٔلُ عَن ذَنۢبِهِۦٓ إِنسٌ وَلَا جَآنٌّ ﴿٣٩﴾
فَبِأَىِّ ءَالَآءِ رَبِّكُمَا تُكَذِّبَانِ ﴿٤٠﴾
يُعْرَفُ ٱلْمُجْرِمُونَ بِسِيمَٰهُمْ فَيُؤْخَذُ بِٱلنَّوَٰصِى وَٱلْأَقْدَامِ ﴿٤١﴾
فَبِأَىِّ ءَالَآءِ رَبِّكُمَا تُكَذِّبَانِ ﴿٤٢﴾

Final phase in the existence of the human beings of all the worlds is of the actual day of reward and punishment. Some will go to hell and some to the paradise. On this the verses 55(44-47) says:—

This is the Hell which the sinners deny,
In its midst and in the midst of boiling
hot water will they wander round,
Then which of the favours of your Lord
will ye deny?
But for such as fear, the time when they
stand before their Lord,
There will be two Gardens,
Then which of the favours of your Lord
ye will deny"
.....55(44–47)

هَٰذِهِۦ جَهَنَّمُ ٱلَّتِى يُكَذِّبُ بِهَا ٱلْمُجْرِمُونَ ﴿٤٣﴾
يَطُوفُونَ بَيْنَهَا وَبَيْنَ حَمِيمٍ ءَانٍ ﴿٤٤﴾
فَبِأَىِّ ءَالَآءِ رَبِّكُمَا تُكَذِّبَانِ ﴿٤٥﴾
وَلِمَنْ خَافَ مَقَامَ رَبِّهِۦ جَنَّتَانِ ﴿٤٦﴾
فَبِأَىِّ ءَالَآءِ رَبِّكُمَا تُكَذِّبَانِ ﴿٤٧﴾

The Prophet of Allah says:

Narrated Ibn Umar رضی اللہ عنہ **:Alla's Apostle (S.A.W.) said, "If Allah sends punishment upon a nation it befalls upon the whole population indiscriminately and then they will be resurrected (and judged) according to their deeds'"**

Chapter—3

CATASTROPHIC EVENTS AND MORAL DEGRADATION

Lo! Allah wrongs not even of the weight of an ant;
And if there is a good deed,
He will double it,
And will give (the doer) from,
His presence the immence reward"
......4(40).

إِنَّ اللَّهَ لَا يَظْلِمُ مِثْقَالَ ذَرَّةٍ وَإِن تَكُ حَسَنَةً يُضَاعِفْهَا وَيُؤْتِ مِن لَّدُنْهُ أَجْرًا عَظِيمًا

It is a radical concept which the one, who has a pure materialistic approach of life, would find it difficult to grasp; but Holy Quran leads us to the new dimension of thought that national catastrophies are generally, initiated by the moral degradation of nations. When a society degrades and decays to a degree that it looses all its utility for a moral civilization, then its doomsday is hastened on it, and ultimately, it is wiped out of the physical framework of life also. Holy Quran enumerates various historical account of the nations which had defied the moral social laws of human civilization, that is they rebelled against the code of life given to mankind by their Creator, which through His immense bounty, He has been clarifying for them throughout ages by sending His messengers, time and again. As nations degrade morally, in the first instance, they are served with minor warnings so that they may understand and mend their ways. In the end, when they reach the point of no return, the process of accountability is accelerated and they are destroyed through some catastrophic natural disastors. Examples of such catastrophies are, large scale epidemics, national quarrels, social disorders and wars, earthquakes volcanoes, meteorities and other natural agents which destroy immoral nations thus setting in their premature Doomsdays. Following revelations illustrate such type of punishments which had fallen on people in the past:

"And We sent Noah to his people, and
He lived with them,
A thousand years minus fifty,
Then they were caught by deluge,
For they were evil"
. . . **29/14**

﴿١٤﴾ وَلَقَدْ أَرْسَلْنَا نُوحًا إِلَىٰ قَوْمِهِۦ
فَلَبِثَ فِيهِمْ أَلْفَ سَنَةٍ إِلَّا خَمْسِينَ
عَامًا فَأَخَذَهُمُ ٱلطُّوفَانُ وَهُمْ ظَٰلِمُونَ

"To Midian We sent their brother Shuaib,
He said, O,people, worship God,
And be ready for the Day of Resurrection,
Do not evil and
create not mischief in the land;
But they denied him and (ultimately)
were seized by an earthquake,
and lay overturned in their homes
in the morning"
. . . **29/37**

﴿٣٦﴾ وَإِلَىٰ مَدْيَنَ أَخَاهُمْ شُعَيْبًا فَقَالَ
يَٰقَوْمِ ٱعْبُدُوا۟ ٱللَّهَ وَٱرْجُوا۟ ٱلْيَوْمَ ٱلْءَاخِرَ
وَلَا تَعْثَوْا۟ فِى ٱلْأَرْضِ مُفْسِدِينَ
﴿٣٧﴾ فَكَذَّبُوهُ فَأَخَذَتْهُمُ ٱلرَّجْفَةُ
فَأَصْبَحُوا۟ فِى دَارِهِمْ جَٰثِمِينَ

"And Aad & Thamud,
It will be clear to you from their habitation,
(How they were destroyed)
For Satan had made their deeds look
attractive to them,
And turned them away from the path,
And yet were a people of acument"
. . . .**29/38**

﴿٣٨﴾ وَعَادًا وَثَمُودَا۟ وَقَد تَّبَيَّنَ لَكُم مِّن
مَّسَٰكِنِهِمْ وَزَيَّنَ لَهُمُ ٱلشَّيْطَٰنُ
أَعْمَٰلَهُمْ فَصَدَّهُمْ عَنِ ٱلسَّبِيلِ وَكَانُوا۟
مُسْتَبْصِرِينَ

Above are only few specific examples of nations in the past who degraded in evil and were finally overtaken by the natural process of accountability and destroyed. In the following a general account of different modes of punishment is given which in the past had brought the premature doom of the immoral nations.

"And We seized all of them (the wrongdoers);
Against some We sent a violent wind
hurling stones.
And some We submerged under earth,
And some We drowned,
It was not for God to wrong them,
But they wronged against themselves"
. . . **29/40**

﴿٤٠﴾ فَكُلًّا أَخَذْنَا بِذَنۢبِهِۦ فَمِنْهُم مَّنْ أَرْسَلْنَا
عَلَيْهِ حَاصِبًا وَمِنْهُم مَّنْ أَخَذَتْهُ ٱلصَّيْحَةُ
وَمِنْهُم مَّنْ خَسَفْنَا بِهِ ٱلْأَرْضَ وَمِنْهُم
مَّنْ أَغْرَقْنَا وَمَا كَانَ ٱللَّهُ لِيَظْلِمَهُمْ
وَلَٰكِن كَانُوٓا۟ أَنفُسَهُمْ يَظْلِمُونَ

Type of catastrophies highlighted in the above quoted verses sometime do happen now also. If there were a prophet, he could clearly tell us, what initiated them? In this connection the last part of the verse 40(29) is however, very revealing that punishment of societies is due to their own fault. God wrongs not. Nation can go on living a happly life, provided they keep following the natural social and moral laws; expounded by the prophets of Allah; and for us have been very clearly preserved in the Holy Quran. Most of the ills in the world should be traceable to man's own doings;

٧٩ مَّآ أَصَابَكَ مِنْ حَسَنَةٍ فَمِنَ ٱللَّهِ
وَمَآ أَصَابَكَ مِن سَيِّئَةٍ فَمِن نَّفْسِكَ

Whatever of good befalls thee,
It is from Allah,
And whatever of ill befalls thee,
It is from thyself. . . . .4(79)

Catasrophies and Moral Reasons.

From the above we can say that spiritual and moral degradation actually becomes the cause of misfortunes of nations. Going into details of the relevant verses, it appears, that even natural phenomenon like earthquakes, floods, huricanes meteor showers etc. are sometimes caused by the spiritual and moral reasons. In the domain of cause and effect this is a revolutionary concept.

In the normal scientific approach, the reasons for any event are traced to the physical laws. But in the above we have seen a new dimension in the study of events. Accordingly we can say that all events are governed by two types of causes i.e. Spiritual and physical causes. Spiritual causes are governed by the spiritual laws, and physical causes are determined by the physical laws. In this approach Quran also leads us to the conclusion that spiritual causes precede the physical causes. In other words we can say that physics cannot be separated from the metaphysics. In fact metaphysics leads the physics. According to this philosphy occurance of events may be represented as follows:—

Meta Physics + Physics → Events
or Moral Causes + Physical causes → Events

According to this scheme of things, we may say that events first get shape in the minds of people; filthy minds give birth to the filthy events, healthy minds give birth to the healthy events. In this respect the Holy Quran says that you cannot change your state unless you change what is hidden in your kinds; .

Lo! Allah changes not the condition of a folk untill,
They first change that which is in their hearts"
. . . . .13(11)

إِنَّ ٱللَّهَ لَا يُغَيِّرُ مَا بِقَوْمٍ
حَتَّىٰ يُغَيِّرُوا مَا بِأَنفُسِهِمْ

Science today, satisfies itself in its search of physical reasons. But from the Holy Quran we gather that there is a force beyond the physics also which actually governs and controls the physical laws. This force is motivated by the mind force, which in turn pends on the deeds of the people. There is the mind of individual, and on the whole, there is also the collective mind of the society. Sum total of the individual minds is equal to the mind of the society i.e.

Mind of the Society = Σ individual minds

Thus there is a mysterious communication between the physical and spiritual laws, i.e. between the matter and the mind. When mind desires something matter begins to react. For example when a person makes up his mind, first of all matter in his body takes the command of the mind. The matter around and coming in the way of his desire begins to adopt itself to the mind of the individual. On the larger-scale, the mind of the society shapes the matter in a larger way also. Mind of the world is the sum total of the mind of the societies and collectively it modifies the world affairs. Thus relationship of meta-physics and physics it is like the master-slave relationship. Physics is slave to the Metaphysics.

ΣMind of societies $\longrightarrow$Mind of the world.

Quran also guides us that mind is the characteristics of human soul. Immoral thoughts and deeds corrupt the soul and degrade the mind, which ultimately, to escape further frustration, tension and immorality, may trigger the physical laws to its own destruction. In this regard it may choose a well planned suicide, or an un-planned accident, it matters little. The materialistics then sit down to investigate the cause of the catastrophy in terms of physical laws, and assign the causes to such and such physical reasons; ignoring what had actually caused those physical reasons to happen. Perhaps it was due to a sick soul of the individual or of the society which had masterminded the physical forces to obey and cause the happening. Next time let us also look for the metaphysical reasons besides the physical reasons which trigger the events.

A relationship between the Metaphysical causes and physical causes is shown in Fig-4, according to which the former precedes and on reaching a critical limit triggers the later. This also explains the fact that in his various sayings the Prophet of Allah had told that near the Doomsday, moral degradation would be at its climax, meaning that under the command of Allah these could become the cause of affictions on the people of earth appearing in the form of wars, and natural catastrophes. such as earthquakes, volcanoes and fires etc.

Narrated Abdullah and Abu Musa: The Prophet (S.A.W.) said, 'Near the establishment of the Hour there will be days during which Religious ignorance will spread, knowledge will be taken away (vanish) and there will be much Al-Harj, and Al-Harj means killing '.

Narrated Abu Huraira: The Prophet (S.A.W.) said, "Time will pass rapidly because of indulging in the pleasures of the world and forgetting one's duties towards Allah, good deeds will decrease, miserliness will be thrown (in the hearts of the people) afflictions will appear and there will be much "Al-Harj". They said, 'O Allah's Apostle! What is Al-Harj?" He said, 'Killing ! Killing!".

A further explanation of the Hypothesis that metaphysics precedes physics or the physical causes are triggered by the metaphysical reasons, may be seen in the Chapter 18 of this book, which put up the theory that each atom is not only a stable particle of matter but also the basic living unit having an elementary mind of its own. Thus atom is not a lifeless building block of matter but an integration of, life, mass and mind, which together control the behaviour and characteristics of elements, following the laws of nature framed by God, which are in built in their internal memory. All reactions follow the mechanics of the natural laws. Since human beings possess the most developed minds, therefore they can interact with matter directly through physics or indirectly through metaphysics via minds of things. Vice-versa, things get effected by the spirtual inclinations of human beings for their good or bad. In other words metaphysics in the environment effects the physics of the world around i.e. metaphysical causes precede the physical causes.

Fig.4.

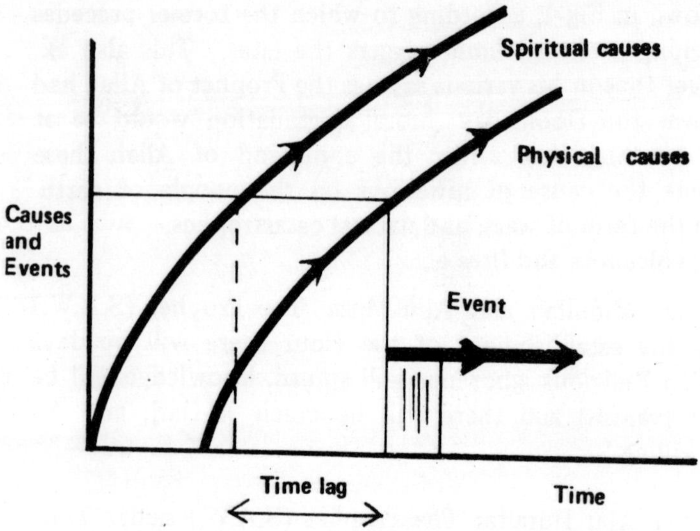

Spiritual causes trigger the Physical cause which then generate the events. In this chain human mind is the primover of the individual, society and the world. Mind power can overtake the Physical forces. Things first shape in the minds of people. Minds shapes the behaviour; Behaviour shapes the events. Thus spiritual causes precede the physical causes. There is however a time lag between the both. Events trigger as the spiritual causes exceed a critical dimension. Nature of the events depend upon the state of mind. Change for the good need good minds. Evil would only breed destruction and wrath of God.

Spiritual causes————→Physical causes
Pjysical causes————→Events
Events————————→Consequences.

The hypothesis that Physical causes follow the spiritual causes is derivalike from the following Quranic revelation.
"Lo! Allah changes not the condition of a folk, until they (first, change that of which is in their hearts".....13(11)

Chapter—4.

MECHANICS OF THE UNIVERSAL DOOMSDAY

"Allah originates creation,
then He reverts them ,
In the end, you will go back to Him"
. . . .30(11)

﴿١١﴾ ٱللَّهُ يَبْدَؤُا۟ ٱلْخَلْقَ ثُمَّ يُعِيدُهُۥ ثُمَّ
إِلَيْهِ تُرْجَعُونَ

Universal Doomsday is the event when the entire order of the present existence will come to an end and change into altogether a new order of existence. Day of Resurrection (يوم الدين) follows it. According to the current scientific thought most cosmologists also favour the idea that universe is not for ever; that sometime in the remote past it had a distinct beginning and some day, it will end itself. Thereafter, a new beginning will take place. Thus latest scientific thought is moving to the Quranic concept of Universal Doomsday, to be discussed in this chapter.

SCIENTIFIC EVIDENCE

On this, scientific evidence[13,29,31] is that at present universe is expanding but its rate of expansion is steadily falling, as gravity restrains the dispersal of the galaxies; so one day it will come to a halt. As we will see later in this paper, this agrument is also very much in line with the Quranic revelations 21(104), 51(47). Time period of this change over depends on the density of universe. Change over from the expansion to the contraction is attributed to the unseen material such as neutrinos and black holes, as well as unseen energy such as gravity waves. Since it is almost impossible to assess the overall density of universe, therefore it is virtually impossible to predict the timing of the reversal also.[13]

However once the universe comes to a halt, it will begin to contract in a manner that is the time reflection of its expansion phase. At first the contraction will be slow, but gradually the pace will accelerate. Galaxies that are now receding from one another will start to approach toward each other, gathering speed all the time. That will set the stage for a monstrous cataclysm.

According to Paul Davies[10] when the universe has shrunk to an hundredth of its present size, the compression effect will have elevated the temperature to the boiling point of water; and the earth (if it has survived the sun's death) will become uninhabitable. An observer would no longer be able to distinguish individual galaxies, for these would, by now, have begun to merge with each other as the intergalactic spaces close up. Further shrinkage will raise the temperature to the point where the sky itself will begin to glow like a furnace. Probably Holy Quran refers to this phase when it says:—

يَوْمَ تَكُونُ السَّمَآءُ كَالْمُهْلِ ﴿٨﴾

That is the Day when;
"The heaven will look like,
The molten pot of copper"
... 70(8)

In the receding universe[10], stars, embedded in the white hot space, will start to boil, then explode. The pace of events now quickens. All structures are vaporized and their atoms dispersed, in a few hundred thousand years or more, the very nuclei are themselves smashed to pieces in the escalating temperatures. The time scale of events now becomes frantic. The universe is shrinking appreciably in minutes, then seconds, then microseconds. Finally the cosmic contraction ends into an uncontrolled implosion, "Big Crunch", setting the pace for a rebeginning.

The Big Crunch is like the Big Bang in reverse[34]. In it nuclear particles break apart into quarks, all manner of subnuclear splinters are created but, in the twinkling of an eye, the entire universe shrivels into less than the space of an atom, where upon, space-time also disintegrate into the "Singularity".

Many physicists believe that the "Big Crunch" represents the end of the physical universe. Just as they believe the universe i.e. all space, time and matter; came into existence in a "Big Bang" so they believe it goes out of existence in a Big Crunch. This is total annihilation. Nothing is left. No places, no moments, no things. This is the final "Singularity" as all of existence succumbs to the infinite destruction. In the words of Paul Davies, gravity, the midwife of the cosmos, is also its undertaker. Holy Quran also guides us to a similar state of the End, though the concept of scientific singularity does not represent its concept of God:—

Fig.5: Scenario of the creation of Universe.

Subject of the Doomsday is closely connected with the creation of universe. Greeks thought that universe had always existed an idea which figures out in the modern theory of steady state universe, postulated by Fred Hoyle. But this has been superceded by the more widely accepted theory by George Gamow, that universe had a beginning and has started with a great explosion called Big Bang; now it may last for ever. A modification to the Big Bang theory is the pulsating universe theory, that universe keeps on repeating itself. Lattest views were summed up by Stephen Hawking in 1983 that universe started with a Big Bang, it will fold itself back to its origin and from there on, would restart in an exponential manner. This view is nearer to the Quranic concept of the creation of universe.

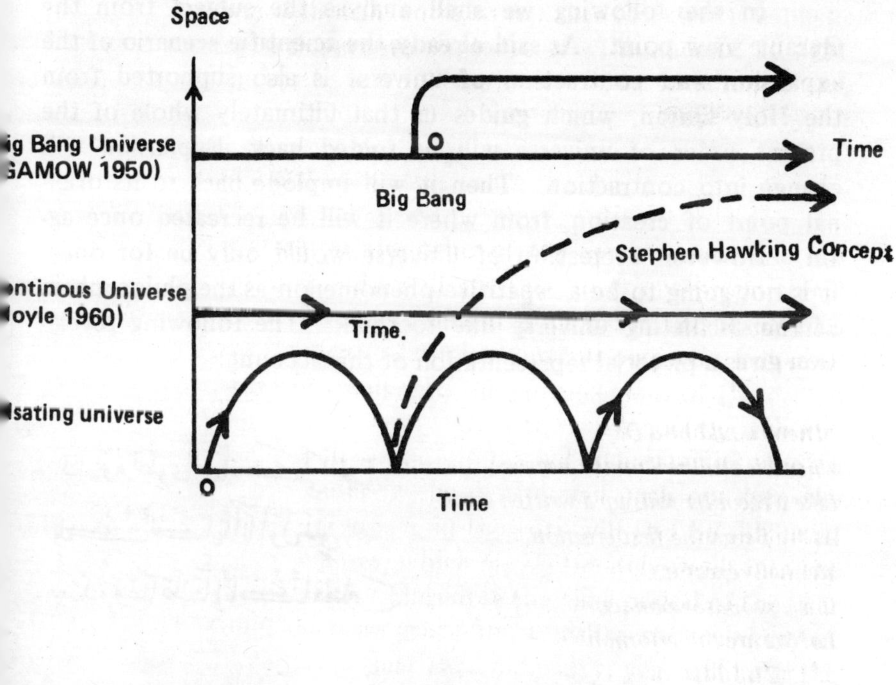

"All that is there will perish,
Except the Face of your Lord,
Full of Majesty, Bounty and Honour"
. . . .55(26-27)

٢٦- كُلُّ مَنْ عَلَيْهَا فَانٍ
٢٧- وَيَبْقَىٰ وَجْهُ رَبِّكَ
ذُو الْجَلَالِ وَالْإِكْرَامِ

However not all scientists[10] are prepared to accept this spectacular demise of the universe. Some also argue that unknown physical forces will cause the Big Crunch to stop at some fantastic density, causing the universe to 'bounce' back again into another cycle of expansion and reconstruction, followed by another and another, and so on, and infinitum. However, Holy Quran does not seem to favour this type of repetition.

QURANIC VIEW POINT

In the following we shall analyse the subject from the Quranic view point. As said already, the scientific scenario of the expansion and contraction of universe is also supported from the Holy Quran, which guides us that ultimately whole of the present order of universe will be folded back. Expansion will change into contraction. Then it will implode back to its original point of creation, from where it will be recreated once again. However, recreation of universe would only be for once. It is not going to be a repetitive phenomenon as the philosophers of the oscillating universe like to think[5]. The following revelation gives a pictorial representation of this account:--

"There would be a Day,
When We shall roll up the heavens,
Like a recorder rolls up a written scroll,
As We began the first creation,
We shall repeat it,
It is a promise upon us,
Lo! We are to perform it"
. . . . .21(104)

١٠٤ يَوْمَ نَطْوِي السَّمَاءَ كَطَيِّ السِّجِلِّ
لِلْكُتُبِ ۚ كَمَا بَدَأْنَا أَوَّلَ خَلْقٍ
نُّعِيدُهُ ۚ وَعْدًا عَلَيْنَا ۚ إِنَّا كُنَّا فَاعِلِينَ

This is the general principle for all type of doomsdays. In the case of universal catastrophe, this verse indicates that one day it will begin to contract and so it will be brought back to its original point of creation.

Fig.6. The Quranic concept of creation of universe.

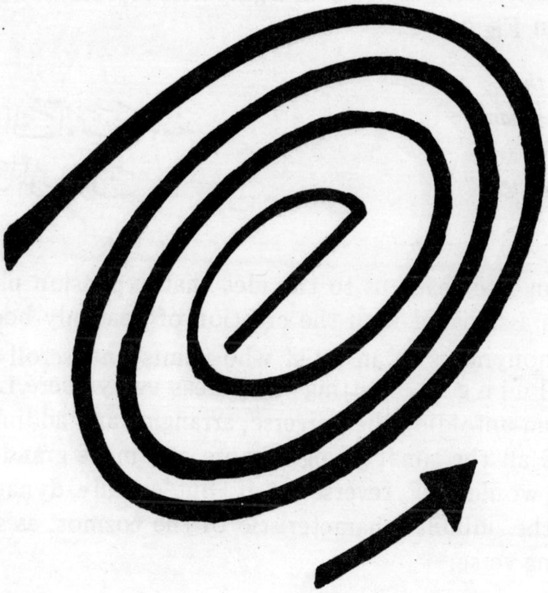

"And We Built the Heaven,
with Twist of the "Divine' Hand"

٤٧- وَالسَّمَآءَ بَنَيْنٰهَا بِاَيْيدٍ
وَّاِنَّا لَمُوْسِعُوْنَ ○

and;

"We surely are Expanding it"
. . . . 51(47)

In the Quranic concept of universe the pre-universe state consisted of a concentrated core of light energy which grew with time. As it approached supercriticality, it exploded with a Big Bang as if God parted off nothingness into the pair of matter and anti-matter. Since then, it is expanding and rotating. This original spin has given birth to the rotary motion of the galaxies and individual heavenly bodies, down to the very core of the atom. Finally universe will begin to contract and fold back to the original shape. Then it will explode again to give birth to a much bigger universe. The overall scenario of the creation, evolution and end of universe as soon through the Holy Quran by your author is shown in the fig. 9.

As for the expansion state of the universe, the following revelation provides a clear indication, a graphical representation of which is shown in Fig.6

"We created it with the
Twist of the (Divine) Hand,
and
Surely We are expanding it"
....51(47)

٤٧ وَٱلسَّمَآءَ بَنَيْنَٰهَا بِأَيْيدٍ
وَإِنَّا لَمُوسِعُونَ

Holy Quran also leads us to the idea that expansion phase of the universe is associated with the creation of heavenly bodies 55(7). This is synonymous to an artist who paints on a scroll and goes on unfolding it, putting new ideas everywhere. Likewise, God has been unfolding the universe, arranging and adding to it new creations all the time, giving it more and more grandeur. Folding process would be reverse of it, but equally dynamic, which is infact the inbuilt characteristic of the cosmos, as seen from the following verse:—

"Everyday, is a day of
New splendour,
For (your Lord)"
...55(29)

٢٩ يَسْـَٔلُهُۥ مَن فِى ٱلسَّمَٰوَٰتِ وَٱلْأَرْضِ ۚ كُلَّ يَوْمٍ
هُوَ فِى شَأْنٍ

Recent discoveries in the working of the cosmos are a witness of the fact expressed in this verse. There is going on, a very busy schedule of creation, re-creation and disposal of the millions of solar systems, all the time in the heavens. Thus everyday is a day of new splendour in the universe. Even the contraction phase which may be termed as the gradual process of decommissioning of the universe, is going to be a highly dynamic phase of existence marked with the fire works of exploding stars all around.

The folding process of universe indicated in the verse 21(104) can be imagined to occur in many ways. As discussed earlier, currently popular scientific hypothesis is that there possibly exists a large amount of unseen hidden matter in space, which will put it into contraction phase.[13] It will be caused by the force of gravity which always tries to pull things inward. A stage is expected to reach when the gravitational pull of the invisible

According to the Holy Quran, universe is not open but closed one, which is not for ever. There was a time when it was created and since then it has been evolving. In the end, the Creator will fold it back to its original singularity. Then He will recreat it into a much bigger and more manoificent univrse which will then be an open universe never to end again. · Graphical representation of this phenominon is given below.

Expansion of universe is analogus to dots on baloon when inflated the dots rush apart and when deflated they rush into.

About the phenomenon of first expansion and then contraction the Holy Quran says,

"REMEMBER THE DAY
WHEN WE SHALL ROLL UP THE HEAVEN
AS A RECORDER ROLLS UP A SCROLL
LIKEWISE WE BEGAN THE FIRST CREATION
SURELY WE ARE GOING TO REPEAT IT"
. . . .21(104).

Fig.7

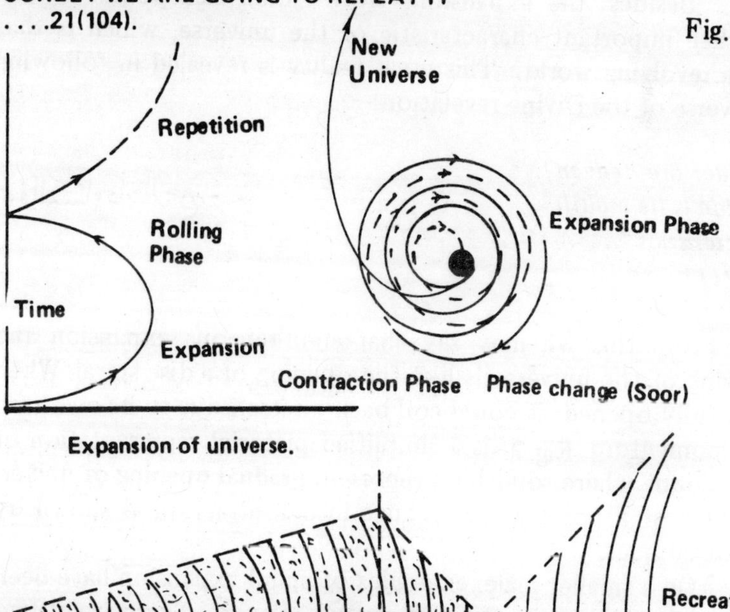

Expansion of universe.

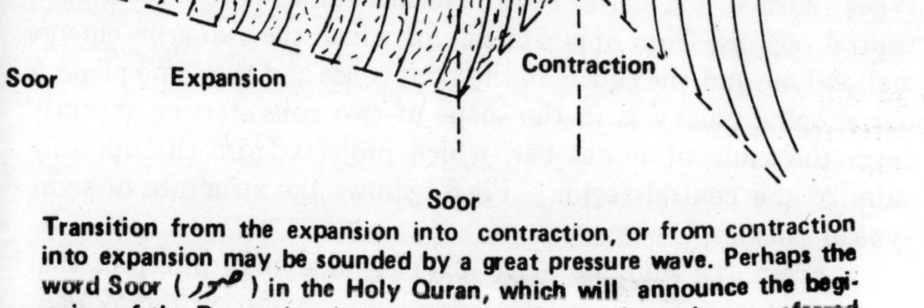

Transition from the expansion into contraction, or from contraction into expansion may be sounded by a great pressure wave. Perhaps the word Soor (صور) in the Holy Quran, which will announce the beginning of the Doomsday, is synonmous with the phase change referred above.

matter exceeds the expanding forces and changes the expansion into contraction. Neutrinos, which are extremely small particles of matter, having mass less than electrons, are thought to be the principal component of this invisible matter. However, the biggest possible brake to the universe could be due to the massless wells of pure Gravity i.e. blackholes, the number and size of which can never be known in the universe. When they open their mouths to swallow the matter, universe would collapse back much earlier than the science at present may think off.

SPIRAL TYPE OF EXPANSION AND CONTRACTION OF UNIVERSE

Besides the expansion, Holy Quran also points toward an other important characteristic of the universe, which is that it is a revolving world. This great reality is revealed in following brief verse of the Divine revelation:—

(Consider the heaven)
Rotation is its inbuilt
characteristics"
... 86(11).

وَٱلسَّمَآءِ ذَاتِ ٱلرَّجْعِ ⑪

From this we may say that simultaneous expansion and revolving of the universe is like the opening of a disc spiral. When it has fully opened, it could coil back on itself due to its own residual momentum. Fig.7 is a simplified pictorial representation of this account where solid lines represent gradual opening of universe, which at a point would change into contraction as shown by the dotted lines.

On a smaller scale, examples of spiral expansion have been observed in the construction of several galaxies[5]. These are of two types, normal and barrel spiral. Normal spirals have lense-shaped central regions, from opposite side of which the two arms emerge and coil around the centre in the same sense and the same plane. A barrel spiral galaxy is in the shape of two coils starting abruptly from the ends of bright bar, which projects from the opposite sides of the central region. Fig.8 shows the structure of some typical galaxies.

From the Quranic verse 21(104) one may interpret that

Fig.8 Spiral galaxies

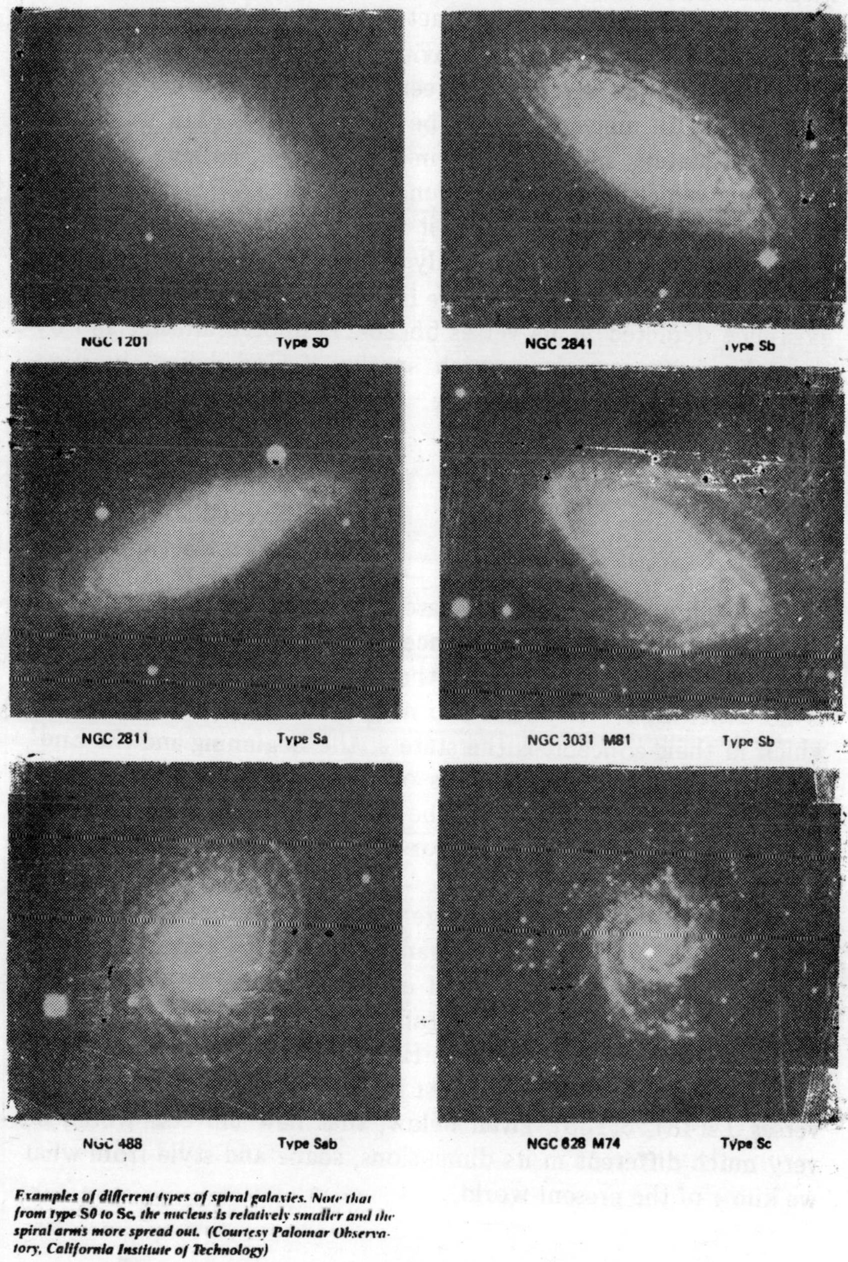

Examples of different types of spiral galaxies. Note that from type S0 to Sc, the nucleus is relatively smaller and the spiral arms more spread out. (Courtesy Palomar Observatory, California Institute of Technology)

universe as a whole may also be of the spiral shape which, after having opened up to its maximum limits, under the influence of its own momentum would coil back on itself. Thus the role of invisible hidden matter in the contraction process of universe may not be the only important factor.

Since pulling force of gravity is inversely proportional to the square of the distance between the bodies, therefore rate of contraction of universe would be much greater than its expansion. Ultimately, all the matter in the universe, rushing in at tremendous velocities from all around, crashes together and annihilated in a fire ball of energy, as it used to be at the outset of the first order of existence. The only Reality then would remain of God alone. In the Holy Quran we find these two extreme states of existence depicted in its verses 55(26-27) quoted already and by the following verse also, which speaks of God, being the First and the Last Reality of Existence:—

"He is the First, and
He is the Last"
. . . .57(3)

هُوَ الْأَوَّلُ وَالْآخِرُ ٣

Beginning and the End are thus two states of existence when all the secondary existences are terminated into the primary existence of the One and the only One, besides Whom there is no other God. Physicist also now talk of the "Singularity", which in their concept, is the state at the Beginning and the End' of Universe. This Singualirity is of course, not the God of Holy Quran, but, as we see from the verse 57(3), it does manifest the characteristics of the Creator of the universes at the infinity of the Time and Space.[35]

God will then set the stage for a new beginning, for a new world which from the Holy Quran we find to be unimaginably bigger than the present order of universe and which will not reverse again. This would be the fulfilment of the promise of God, made in the verse 21(104), that He will repeat the creation of the universe again. However, it must be interesting to note from the verses 14(48), 3(133), given below, that new universe would be very much different in its dimensions, shape and style from what we know of the present world.

٤٨ يَوْمَ تُبَدَّلُ الْأَرْضُ غَيْرَ الْأَرْضِ
وَالسَّمٰوٰتُ

"On that Day,
When the earth will be ,
changed into another earth;
And the heaven,
(they will be changed also)"
. . . .14(48)

٢١ سَابِقُوٓا۟ إِلَىٰ مَغْفِرَةٍ مِّن رَّبِّكُمْ وَجَنَّةٍ
عَرْضُهَا كَعَرْضِ السَّمَآءِ وَالْأَرْضِ أُعِدَّتْ لِلَّذِينَ
ءَامَنُوا۟ بِاللَّهِ وَرُسُلِهِۦ

"And vie one with another,
for forgiveness from your Lord,
And for a paradise (Jannat),
which is as wide as,
All the heavens and earth (put together),
It is prepared for those who
believe in Allah and His messengers
... 57(21)

Information provided by these verses can be of great scientific interest. Idea that the recreated world is going to be extremely big, so big that even a portion of it will be bigger than the entire order of the present heavens means that it would be much bigger than our universe. , which no doubt is also unimaginably big for us. As per the verse 14(48), the new world would have little resemblance with the present universe. Earth of that universe is just a name in similitude. We cannot know about its real nature and size either, and so also about the other heavenly systems of that world.

Fig.9 VARIOUS STEPS IN THE CREATION, EVOLUTION AND THE END OF UNIVERSE AS SEEN THROUGH THE HOLY QURAN'.28

Phenomenon of creation, evolution and the End of the universe are connected together through the Divine plan. Its end was contained in its creation as the genetic code of a new born is written on its Taqdeer (التقدير) or destiny concerning his life also. The following is a summary of the history of the universe from its Beginning to its End, derived by the author, through his interpretation of the Holy Quran The total scenario looks like a continuous cycle, in which the End is as important a reality as has been the Beginning. The End will be the beginning for a much bigger universe.

I PRE-UNIVERSE

ALLAH.
TIME-SPACE CONTINUUM INTERACTION
↓
BIRTH OF ENERGY-ELEMENTARY MATTER PAIRS
FORMATION OF CONCENTRATED COMPACT CORE
REACHING SUPER CRITICAL
↓
AND BIG BANG
EXTREMELY HIGH PRESSURES AND TEMPERATURES
↓

II EXPANSION PHASE — PRESENT UNIVERSE

CREATION OF DENSER MATTER (SMOKE LIKE STUFF)
BIRTH OF ALL ELEMENTS
↓
EXPANSION AND ROTATION CONTINUES
SPACE FILLED WITH SMOKY STUFF
UNIVERSE EXPANDS TO STABILITY LIMITS
COLD CONDENSATION OF MATTER
BIRTH AND EVOLUTION OF HEAVENLY SYSTEMS

III CLOSING PHASE — UNIVERSE SLOWS DOWN TO CONTRACT

ROTATION AND EXPANSION
CONTINUES
NEW MATTER IS ADDED ALL ALONG
↓
CREATION AND RECREATION OF HEAVENLY
↓
SYSTEMS CONTINUES
NEW MATTER ACTS AS BRAKE TO EXPANSION
ROTATION AND EXPANSION KEEP ON SLOWING
ADDITIONAL MATTER OVER GROWS TO STOP EXPANSION
UNIVERSE BEGINS TO FOLD BACK
CONTRACTION CONTINUES
UNIVERSE REVERSES TO POINT SOURCE
IMPLODES
↓

IV NEW ORDER

AN OTHER BIG BANG
A MUCH MUCH BIGGER UNIVERSE IS REBORN
BEGINNING OF A NEW AND MORE SPLENDID UNIVERSE

Chapter-5.

SOME EVENTS OF THE UNIVERSAL DOOMSDAY

We have already discussed that beginning of Universal Doomsday would be marked by the phase change from expansion into contraction. This transient would be so powerful that it would be felt everywhere in the whole of the cosmos. It has been denoted by the word SOOR (صُوْر) in the Holy Quran, which will spread a wave of terror throughout the universe. Verse 27(87) has pointed out this awful reality in the following words:—

"And (remind them of) the Day,
When the Soor will be blown,
And all who are in the heavens and
the earth, will stare in terror,
Save him whom Allah wills,
And, all come to Him humbled"
. . . .27(87)

وَيَوْمَ يُنفَخُ فِي ٱلصُّورِ فَفَزِعَ مَن فِي
ٱلسَّمَٰوَٰتِ وَمَن فِي ٱلْأَرْضِ إِلَّا مَن شَآءَ ٱللَّهُ ۚ
وَكُلٌّ أَتَوْهُ دَٰخِرِينَ ٨٧

Thus Soor (صُوْر) will sound the start of the Universal Doomsday. It will be a tremendous event, shaking everyone, everywhere. Thereafter things will be changing from bad to worse. The Quran has called it a "Heavy Day" in the heavens and earth; a day of chaos and turbulance:—

"It is a heavy Day,
In the heavens and earth"
. . . . 7(187)

هُوَ ثَقُلَتْ فِي ٱلسَّمَٰوَٰتِ وَٱلْأَرْضِ ۚ

We also see in the Holy Quran that at the initiation of the Doomsday, control mechanism of the universe will be let loose, stars will burst, planets will crash into one another. In that state, cosmos will be filled with a smoky stuff. Following verses illustrate the state of turmoil on that day:—

"And the heaven will be split asunder,
And the Stars dispersed".
. . . .82(1-2).

إِذَا ٱلسَّمَآءُ ٱنفَطَرَتْ ١
وَإِذَا ٱلْكَوَاكِبُ ٱنتَثَرَتْ ٢

Splitting asunder of heaven (تَشَقَّقُ السَّمَاءُ) may mean the break of the order and stability, among the various components of the universe. The verse 25(25) reflects the same idea in the following words:—

"A Day, when the heaven. *splits asunder* *With a dazzling white cloud,* *And the angels ascend in continuous stream"* *....25(25)*	٢٥ وَيَوْمَ تَشَقَّقُ السَّمَآءُ بِالْغَمَامِ وَنُزِّلَ الْمَلٰٓئِكَةُ تَنزِيلًا

The use of words (تَشَقَّقُ) meaning spliting asunder in the verse, 82(1-2), seems to signify that holding forces will then not be enough to keep balance in the heavenly bodies. Heavenly clouds in the verse 25(25) is taken to mean the cosmic gaseous matter constituting galactic worlds, which now tend to cluster together to give birth to heavenly system, Near the Doomsday it would start diffusing out disorderly. The use of the word earth in the verses describing the ultimate Doomsday is not to be taken necessarily for our earth, only. This word applies to all earth-like-bodies everywhere in the cosmos which can support life and have living beings like us. All these worlds would have their doomsday at their turn, but much before the Universal Doomsday.

In the following are given some more verses which describe the state of overall disorder in the universe at the time of the Doomsday:—

"On that Day, *Heaven will heave,* *with awful heavings* *and the mountains;* *They will fly hither and* *thither"* *.....52(9-10)*	٩ يَوْمَ تَمُورُ السَّمَآءُ مَوْرًا ١٠ وَتَسِيرُ الْجِبَالُ سَيْرًا

In this verse heaving of the heaven signify the scene of an overall break of order in the universe. Flying of mountains seems the state of planets crashing with each other, throwing chunks of matter, roving disorderly in space.

Fig.10. Different Processes for the Death of Stars.

Fig.10-1

Fig.10-2

Fig.10.3

Energy from the nuclear reactions in the core of a supergiant star prevent it from collapsing under the force of its own tremendous gravity. When the nuclear fuel is used up, the core collapses into a neutron star. A shock wave rebounds from the core in a huge explosion, leaving a brightly glowing and expanding cloud, as shown in the Fig. 10.1. The remainder may be a neutron star or a black hole.
Alternately a companion star may become the cause of the Doomsday of a sun also. If one of the stars in a close binary system is a white dwarf (a dense, compact remnant of an ordinary star), its gravity can pull mass from a large companion. When the accumulating mass of the dwarf star reaches an upper limit, a catastrophic contraction begins. The collapsing star ignites in a thermonuclear explosion & is destroyed.

The following verses seem to refer to the abnormal outbursts in the form of supernovae when stars will fall off their stable positions, crash into each other and so loose their energy reactions causing gradual darkness allaround;

(Watch for the Day)
When the Sun is folded up,
When the stars fall,
(from their stable positions),
Loosing their light"
....81(1-2)

١ إِذَا ٱلشَّمْسُ كُوِّرَتْ
٢ وَإِذَا ٱلنُّجُومُ ٱنكَدَرَتْ

"And when the heaven
It is torn apart"
....81(11)

١١ وَإِذَا ٱلسَّمَآءُ كُشِطَتْ

These verses reflect a picture of complete chaos and disorder in the universe at the time of its Doomsday. Cause for this disorder is seen in the contraction process of universe discussed already. As the heavenly bodies come closer, the outside gravitational forces may begin to exceed the inward forces holding the plasma of gases in the stars, resulting into release of the external hot gases in space. Due to this, the stars would then tend to expand in volume, gradually reducing the internal pressure low enough to ultimately stop the energy generating nuclear fusion reactions in them. This will make them dull bright, then red and ultimately black bodies without light. Same can also happen through the simple aging process of the stars leading them to their natural death. Fig10 is a sample representation of this phenomena.

The general commotion and chaos, prevailing during the Universal Doomsday is also highlighted by the verses 79(1-6) which reflect the scenario of too much activity of meteors and disorderly motions of stars in space during that period:—

"By those who drag with destruction,
By (the meteors) rushing apart,
By the (lone stars) floating,
By the (angels) hastening,
And those who govern the events
On that day,
Everything that can be in commotion,
Will be in violent commotion,
Commotion after commotion"
... 79(1-6)

١ وَٱلنَّٰزِعَٰتِ غَرْقًا
٢ وَٱلنَّٰشِطَٰتِ نَشْطًا
٣ وَٱلسَّٰبِحَٰتِ سَبْحًا
٤ فَٱلسَّٰبِقَٰتِ سَبْقًا ٥ فَٱلْمُدَبِّرَٰتِ أَمْرًا
٦ يَوْمَ تَرْجُفُ ٱلرَّاجِفَةُ

If we reflect back, the scene depicted in these verses is very much closer to the scientific review of Paul Davies[10] of the contracting universe discussed already. In that state, heavens will appear as a pot of molten copper sizzling, on the furnace as said in the verse 70(8);

"The sky will look as the Molten copper"
...70(8)

٨ يَوْمَ تَكُونُ السَّمَاءُ كَالْمُهْلِ

The analogy of sky looking as molten copper seems to signify the abundance of high-temperature plasma filling the skies, released from the bursting of stars during the last phases of universe. That also signify the break of the identity of individual heavenly bodies. This is the state close enough to the Big Crunch, which will finally announce;

٢٦- كُلُّ مَنْ عَلَيْهَا فَانٍ

٢٧- وَيَبْقَىٰ وَجْهُ رَبِّكَ
ذُو الْجَلَالِ وَالْإِكْرَامِ

All that is there will perish,
Except the Face of your Lord,
Full of Majesty, Bounty and Honour"
...55(26-27)

That will be The end of the present Order of existance to initiate the New Order leading to the Resurrection.

OVERALL SCENERIO

If we summarise the above discussion about the Universal Doomsday the following pictureemergesout from the Holy Quran. In general, it would be the scene of a contracting universe, with everything rushing toward its origin. Cosmos is then full of turbulance; heavenly bodies crashing into each other, stars spewing out hot plasma gases, space filling with smoke, skies littered with debris of heavenly bodies, a state of dreadful commotion all-around. And mankind, anywhere and everywhere, in panic helplessly see their fast approaching Doom. Then there will come the final hour, the Big Crunch, to announce the beginning of a New Order of existence, much more grander than the previous order of universe.

As we review the latest scientific views on this subject we are surprised to find that over centuries science has also been gradually moving to the concepts first pointed out by the Holy Quran. One likes to ask from here, that how is it that a book, given to the world fourteen hundred years ago, could have been the first to expose these scientific ideas? This is especially surprising when we know that Prophet of Allah Whogave it to the world, was neither a scientist, nor was he born in a scientific age. Then how could he had picked up this information from his surroundings? In the face of these realities we are left with no option but to acknowledge that he was inspired from the Creator of the worlds and Quran is the Book from Him for our guidance in this life and the life Here-after . Indeed:—

① يُسَبِّحُ لِلَّهِ مَا فِي السَّمٰوٰتِ وَمَا فِي الْأَرْضِ لَهُ الْمُلْكُ
وَلَهُ الْحَمْدُ وَهُوَ عَلٰى كُلِّ شَيْءٍ قَدِيرٌ
② هُوَ الَّذِي خَلَقَكُمْ فَمِنْكُمْ كَافِرٌ وَمِنْكُمْ مُؤْمِنٌ وَاللَّهُ
بِمَا تَعْمَلُونَ بَصِيرٌ

"All that is in the heavens and
And that is on earth,
Exalts God's limitless Glory,
And to Him all praise is due,
And He has the Power to will anything
He it is Who has created you,
And among you are such as deny this truth
And among you are such as believe (in it).
And God sees all that you do.

③ خَلَقَ السَّمٰوٰتِ وَالْأَرْضَ بِالْحَقِّ وَصَوَّرَكُمْ
فَأَحْسَنَ صُوَرَكُمْ وَإِلَيْهِ الْمَصِيرُ

·He has created the heaven and the earth,
in accordance with (an inner) truth,
and has framed you-framed you so well,
and with Him is your journey's End"
. . .64(1-3)

HADITH:
"Hazrat Abada son of Thabit narrated,
The Prophet of Allah told,
"First of all,
Allah created the Pen and said to it,
"Write, The Pen said,
"What should I write? "Allah told it
to write all that was designed by Him
to happen till the Day of Judgement,
Hence everything is preserved in the
Book of Universe. for ever"
. . . . . TIRMAZI

Fig. 11. An artistic view of the End of Universe:

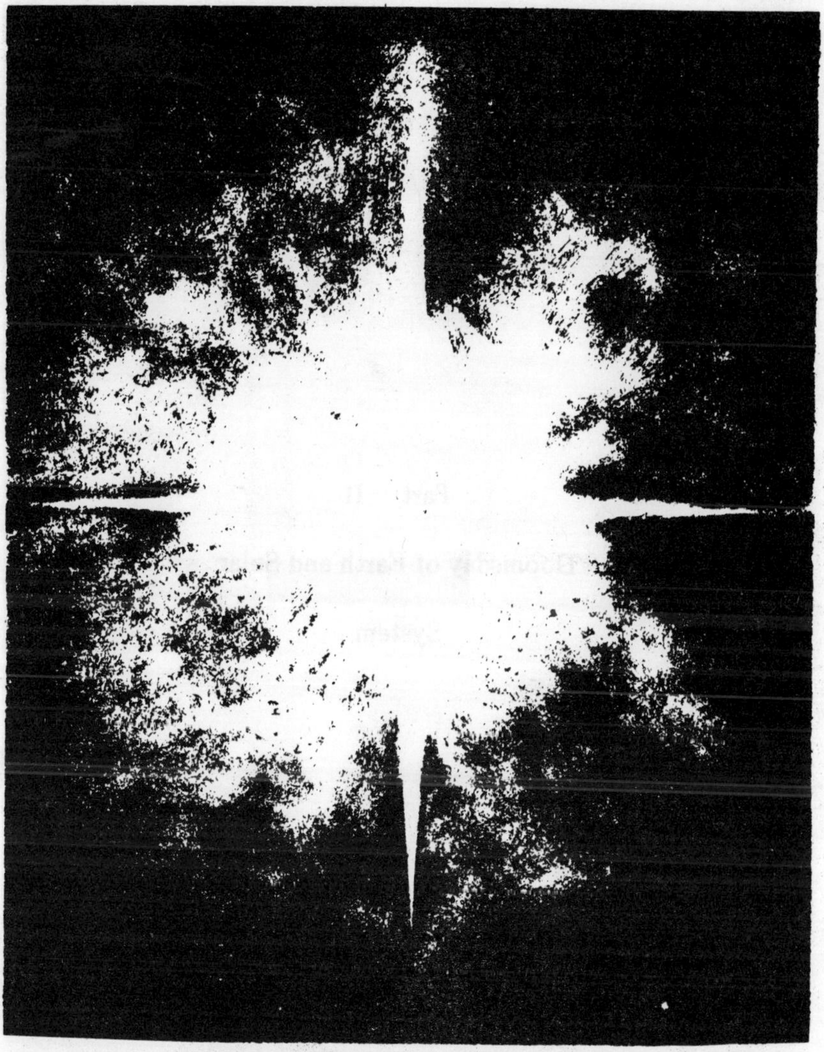

Pre-Universe was an Energy Universe. In its ultimate also, the present universe will be annihilated into the energy state. At that time all material things will loose their existence. Only the energy being should survive. Human soul may also survive, as it is also an energy being.

Universal Doomsday would take its start from the reversal of the expansion of Universe. It will then rush backward to it original point of creation and have a Big Crunch. From there it will re-explode with another Big Bang, to be born again

"And when the heaven splits asunder,
And becomes rosy like red . . . . . .55(37).

Part — II

Doomsday of Earth and Solar System

Chapter-6

STATE OF THE WORLD AFFAIRS NEAR THE EARTHLY DOOMSDAY

Here are two self-explanatory Hadith of the Holy Prophet Muhammad (peace be on him!) regarding the state of world affairs which would prevail near the time of the Earthly Doomsday, and which we can see taking place in the world today.

The translation is as follows:[36]

I. *Ibn Abbas (may Allah be pleased with him!) narrated, "The Holy Prophet (peace be on him!) said, "Prayers will be neglected, carnal desires will be pursued, transgressors will become leaders, it will not be possible to distinguish the truthful from the false, telling lies will become desirable, payment of Zakah will be taken as a burden, the believer will be deemed the most disgraceful and he will be pained at seeing evils (all around) and his heart will melt as salt in water but he will not be able to say anything. Rain will do no good, it will fall out of season. Males will commit adultery with males, and females with females. Women will dominate. The offspring will disobey their parents, friend will treat his friend badly, sins will be taken lightly. Mosques will have external decorations and beauty and there will be worshippers too but there will be hypocrisy and (mutual enmity in their hearts. Then will appear a people from the West* (Maghrib) *who will dominate the weak amongst my people. People will produce (copies of) the Holy Quran in letters of gold but will not act upon it. The: Quran will be recited in a melodious way. Usuary will become rampant. Human blood will have no value, religion will have no helpers. Singing women will be on the increase. The rich will perform the* Hajj *as a pastime, the people of the middle class will do so to conduct business and the poor to beg (for charity)"'. . . .* *(The Mudkhal of Ibn al-Hajj).*

II. *Abu Hurayrah (peace be on him!) reported the Messenger of Allah as saying, "When the booty is taken in turn, property given in trust is treated as spoil, zaka'ah is looked on as a fine, learning is acquired for other than a religious purpose, a man obeys his wife and is unfilial towards his mother, brings his friend near and drives his father far off, voices are reaised in the mosques, the most wicked member of a tribe becomes its ruler, the most worthless member of a people becomes its leader, a man is honoured through fear of the evil he may do, singing girls and string instruments (i.e. modern guitars and pop music) make their appearance, wines are drunk, and the last members of this poeople curse the first ones, look at that time for a violent wind, an earthquake, metamorphosis, pelting rain, and signs following one another like bits of a necklace falling one after the other when its string is cut". (Tirmidhi, Shama el.(Mishkah al-Masabih, Chapter, Fitnah).*

Narrated Abu Huraira Allah Apostle said the Hour will not be established (1) till two big groups fight each other whereupon there will be a great number of casualties on both sides and they will be following one and the same religious doctrine, (2) till about thirty Dajjals (liars) appear, and each one of them will claim that he is Allah's Apostle, (3) till the religious knowledge is taken away (by the death of Religious scholars) (4) earthquakes will increase in number (5) time will pass quickly, (6) afflictions will appear, (7) Al-Harj, (i.e. killing) will increase, (8) till wealth will be in abundance — so abundant that a wealthy person will worry lest nobody should accept his Zakat, and whenever he will present it to someone, that person (to whom it will be offered) will say, "I am not in need of it, (9) till the people compete with one another constructing high buildings, (10) till a man when passing by a grave of someone will say, "Would that I were in his place (11) and till the sun rises from the West. So when the sun will rise and the people will see it (rising from the West) they will all believe (embrace Islam) but that will be the time when: (As Allah said,)

> "No good will it do to a soul to believe then, if it believed not before, nor earned good (by deeds or righteousness) through its Faith". . . .(6:158)

And the Hour will be established while two men spreading a garment in front of them but they will not be able to sell it, nor fold it up.

BUKHARI

Chapter—7

INTRODUCTION TO THE DOOMSDAY OF EARTH AND SOLAR SYSTEM

"Closer and closer to mankind
Comes their reckoning,
Yet they heed not,
And they turn away"
. . . .21(1)

① اقْتَرَبَ لِلنَّاسِ حِسَابُهُمْ وَهُمْ فِي غَفْلَةٍ مُّعْرِضُونَ

Here is a reminder to us that earthly doomsday is not a too far off event, though we are forgetting it We have already discussed in Part-I.that such events are routine phenomena in the universe, which keep falling regularly on individual earthly worlds in the universe, sometimes engulfing the whole of the solar systems also. However it is not necessary that earthly Doomsday and the Solar System Doomsday occur simultaneously. In our case, Quranic wisdom guides us that earthly Doomsday will precede the Doomsday of our solar system. All this will happen according to the general principle of accountability that all worlds have their life periods and when their time comes, no one can avert the catastrophe. The rule is;

"Every event has its
appointed time"
. . . .54(3)

وَكُلُّ أَمْرٍ مُّسْتَقِرٌّ

According to this rule our world must see its Doomsday at its term as a part of the continuous Divine activity of creation, re-creation and accountability. In the universe, there have been many worlds which have already passed through this experience and there are worlds which are passing through it now; and there remain worlds which will meet similar fate in future. This happens according to the Divine law of accountability; that if something looses its purpose of existence or has achieved its design aim, it must give in to the new demands of nature. When this earthly world have fulfilled its purpose of existence it will also be no more needed and destroyed. Flowers wither when they have germinated seed in their wombs.

This is a reality which continually manifests itself in nature.

Fig.12 : **Earth and its place in the Solar System.**

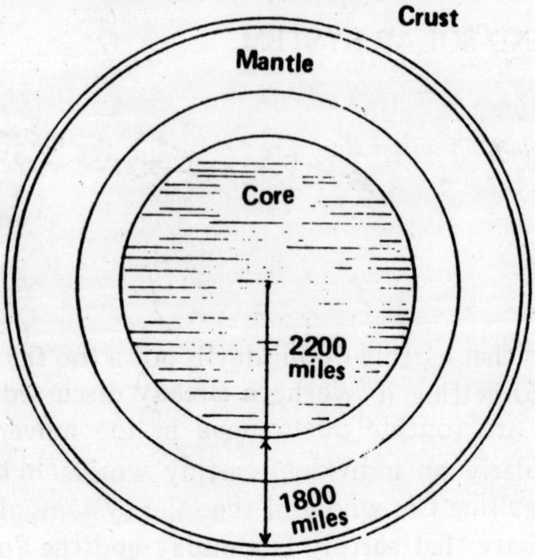

Earth has a core, possibly of iron, highly compressed to a density of 10 to 12 times of water, extending to about half the radious. Then there is a layer of average density of 5.5, which is over 1000 miles thick and overland with a rocky layer, perhaps 700 miles in thickness and density about 4.3. The outer crust is just about 25 miles or so in thickness and seems to float on lower strata. The earth weights about 6,600,000,000,000,000,000,000, tons.

Fig.12-A

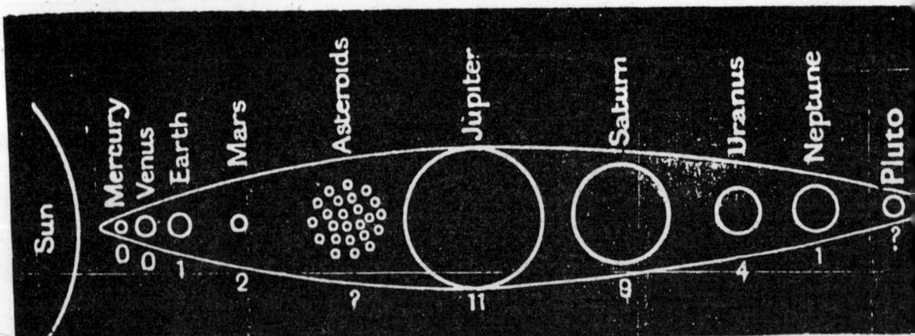

The solar family consist of 9 planets known so far. Earth is one of the smaller planets, situated at a place where temperatures and gravity are just right for the evolution of life.

When it comes to our earth it will not be a unique happening in the universe. It seems from Holy Quran (Ch.22) that life is a widespread phenomena in the cosmos and there are many earth-like bodies populated by living beings who may or may not be like us, but are there. In line with the general principle of accountability, each one of them has to have its Doomsday at its turn. On the same principle we shall have our turn also which is fore told in the verse 55(31) given below:—

They enquire,
" Of Him seek all creatures
in the heavens and earth,
(And) Every Day He manifests
Himself in yet another (wonderous) way
Which, then, of yours sustainer's,
favours can you disavow?
Soon We shall be free to take
you to task also,
O! You twin burden of earth
(men and women)"
.....55(29-31)

٢٩ يَسْأَلُهُ مَنْ فِي السَّمَاوَاتِ وَالْأَرْضِ كُلَّ يَوْمٍ هُوَ فِي شَأْنٍ

٣٠ فَبِأَيِّ آلَاءِ رَبِّكُمَا تُكَذِّبَانِ

٣١ سَنَفْرُغُ لَكُمْ أَيُّهَ الثَّقَلَانِ

The first part of this revelation clearly speaks of other beings in the cosmos. Then it speaks of the dynamism of the other worlds. Then it says that such events are a favour to the beings of the cosmos from the Lord of the Worlds.

Rightly it is so because the continuous upward evolution of universe is made possible through successive generations of stars. In the exploding supernovae due to the very high temperatures and pressures generated at the time of explosion, higher elements and compounds are formed which become the building blocks for the next generations of stars and planets, gradually leading to the creation of life.

The tone of the next sentence indicates the pre-occupation of the Sustainer of the worlds in some similar event at this time somewhere else in the cosmos. Whether it concerns with the Doomsday of an individual earth like bodies or whole of the solar systems it matters little. But it a warning that our turn on earth is soon to come. It is to be realised that orthodox religious scholars tend to make no difference between the earthly Doomsday and the Doomsday of the universe. This is however a simple approach for a complex subject but cannot be said to be wrong either.

Fig.13:

Rushing Through The Universe: Measurements of hundreds of distant galaxies suggest that they are rushing through space at about 400 miles per second, along with the earth and everything else in a vast region. Some astrophysicists believe they may be drawn by the gravitational pull of some huge undiscovered mass, which may bring about their Doomsday when they crash unto it.

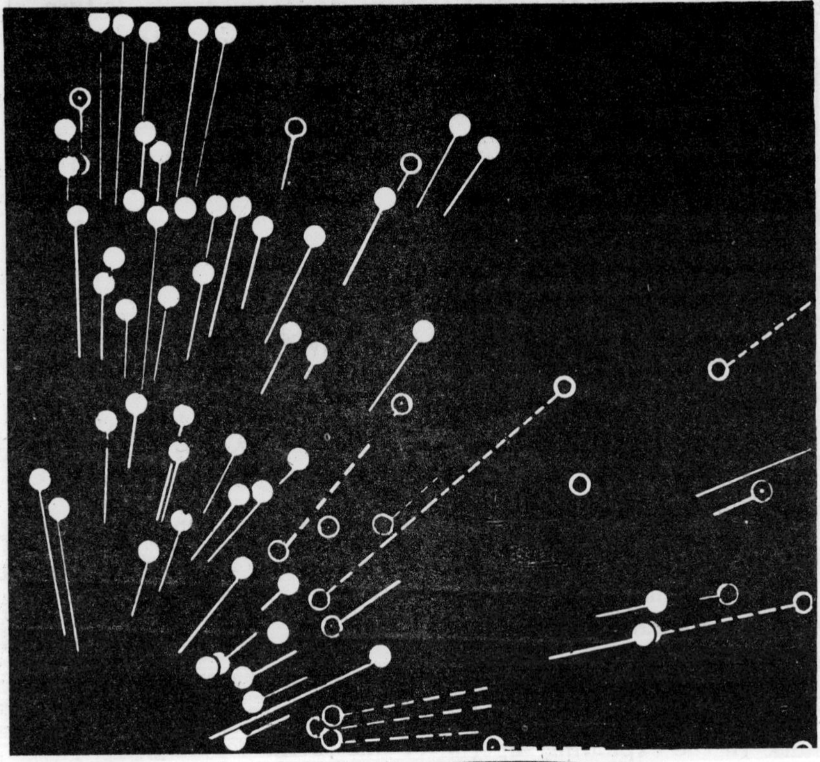

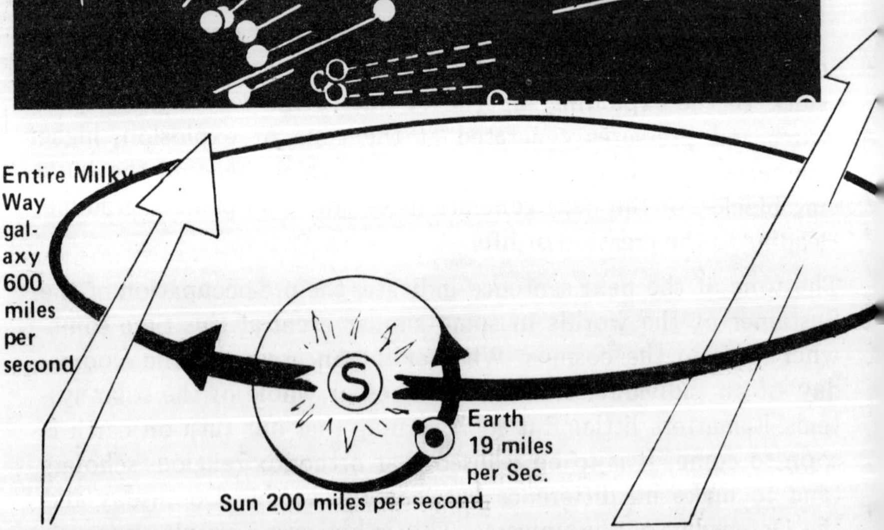

Galaxies Moving En Masse: A sampling of universe: dark circles suggest galaxies moving away from earth. Open ones indicate opposite movement.

Chapter-8.

APPROACH OF THE EARTHLY DOOMSDAY

Let us now investigate the mechanics of the earthly Doomsday in the light of the revealed guidance. It appears from the Holy Quran that coming of the earthly doomsday cannot be predicted by the normal scientific laws. Its knowledge is said to be with God only 7(187); which means that it is not a simple thing which lends itself to precise calculations and analysis. Therefore, it cannot be related to the Doomsday of the Sun also because from its rate of production of energy, and from the amount of hydrogen in it, which is its fuel, it should be scientifically a predictable phenomenon. Following revelations speak about the unpredictability of the earth's Doomsday;

١٨٧ يَسْـَٔلُونَكَ عَنِ ٱلسَّاعَةِ أَيَّانَ
مُرْسَىٰهَا قُلْ إِنَّمَا عِلْمُهَا عِندَ رَبِّى لَا يُجَلِّيهَا
لِوَقْتِهَآ إِلَّا هُوَ ثَقُلَتْ فِى ٱلسَّمَٰوَٰتِ
وَٱلْأَرْضِ لَا تَأْتِيكُمْ إِلَّا بَغْتَةً

"They ask thee of the Hour
(of the Doom),
When shall it come to pass?
Say, knowledge thereof is
with my Lord only,
He alone will manifest it,
At its proper time,
It is heavy in the heaven and earth,
It comes not upon them,
But unaware"
. . . 7(187)

٦٥ قُل لَّا يَعْلَمُ مَن فِى ٱلسَّمَٰوَٰتِ وَٱلْأَرْضِ ٱلْغَيْبَ
إِلَّا ٱللَّهُ وَمَا يَشْعُرُونَ أَيَّانَ يُبْعَثُونَ
٦٦ بَلِ ٱدَّٰرَكَ عِلْمُهُمْ فِى ٱلْءَاخِرَةِ

"None in the heavens and in the earth
Except Allah,
Knows what is hidden,
Nor they can perceive when they
shall be raised up,
Still less, they can comprehend,
The Hereafter"
. . . 27(65-66)

The verses 27(65-66) quoted above also indicate that hidden events (minor and major doomsdays), the event of raising up after death (Resurrection) and the Hereafter (final state of settlement) are distinctly different happenings in the Time-Space **frame**, about which human knowledge will never attain certainty.

The verse 7(187) has made it clear that nature of earthly Doomsday is of the sudden catastrophic event which would take people by surprise. It comes upon them but unaware. The verse 36(49) indicates that this will fall upon them like a blast, giving no time for predictions:—

"They wait not but one blast,
Which will surprise them,
While they are disputing"
. . . .36(49)

٤٩ مَا يَنظُرُونَ إِلَّا صَيْحَةً وَاحِدَةً
تَأْخُذُهُمْ وَهُمْ يَخِصِّمُونَ

Same message is apparent from the verse 16(77);

"And matter of the hour (of Doom),
Is but as twinkling of an eye,
Or it is nearer still,
Lo, Allah is able to do all things"
. . . .16(77)

وَمَآ
أَمْرُ ٱلسَّاعَةِ إِلَّا كَلَمْحِ ٱلْبَصَرِ أَوْ هُوَ أَقْرَبُ ۚ
إِنَّ ٱللَّهَ عَلَىٰ كُلِّ شَىْءٍ قَدِيرٌ

On the question of its timings, the verse 16(77) quoted above gives the impression that it may not be far off. On the relative Possibly it might be the result of some accident in the solar system itself, or an explosion within the body of the earth. The Prophet of Allah illustrated the sudden nature of Doomsday with the example that when it comes, then one who has a piece of bread in his hand, will not have time to put it in his mouth. . . . .(BUKHARI).

On the question of its timings, the verse 16(77) quoted above gives the impression that it is not too far. On the relative astronomical time scale, this is as if the time required to blink an eye but for us even this may be a considerable length of time. According to Muhammad Asad,[14] "the metaphor of the nearness of the Doomsday represents an indefinite length of time. It was frequently expressed by the Prophet of Allah that nearness of the Last Hour is nearness only in comparison with the countless aeons of the past cosmic history". What-ever its nature it would always remain a mystery till the time it falls on earth.

Chapter—9

SIGNS OF THE APPROACHING DOOMSDAY IN THE HOLY QURAN

In the following we shall discuss one of the most interesting feature of the earthly Doomsday which may help us to know something of the pending fate. As said already, although, it is impossible to know exactly about the timings of the Doomsday, yet there are some qualitative indications in the Holy Quran, and in the quotations of the Prophet of Allah, which help us to appreciate its coming. Some of these are given below:—

A HIGH TECHNOLOGY PERIOD

Probably the most prominent indication of the coming of the earthly doomsday given in the Holy Quran is that before the approach of that dreadful event, inhabitants of the earth would have attained a very high degree of technical competency. On this Quran says:—

"(Doomsday would not begin)
Until when the earth,
Puts on its golden adornment
And has been embellished,
And its people think,
They have gained mastery over it,
Then comes down upon it Our Judgement,,
By nigh or by day"
And We cause it to become
(Like) a field mown down,
As if there had been no yesterday"
.....10(24).

حَتّٰىٓ اِذَآ اَخَذَتِ الْاَرْضُ زُخْرُفَهَا
وَازَّيَّنَتْ وَظَنَّ اَهْلُهَآ
اَنَّهُمْ قٰدِرُوْنَ عَلَيْهَآ
اَتٰىهَآ اَمْرُنَا لَيْلًا اَوْ نَهَارًا
فَجَعَلْنٰهَا حَصِيْدًا كَاَنْ لَّمْ . . .
- - - - - - -
تَغْنَ بِالْاَمْسِ كَذٰلِكَ نُفَصِّلُ الْاٰيٰتِ
لِقَوْمٍ يَّتَفَكَّرُوْنَ ○

Muhammad Asad[14] in his commentary of the verse 10(24) says, "they (would) come to believe that they have gained 'mastery over nature' with no conceivable limits to what they may yet achieve. It is to be born in mind that the term 'Zukhruf' (زخرف) bears almost invariably a connotation of artificially, a connotation which in this case is communicated to the subsequent verb "IZZAYYANAT" (وَازَّيَّنَتْ). Thus, the whole of the above parabolic sentence may be understood as alluding to the artificial, illusory 'adornment' brought about by the man stechnological efforts, not in collaboration with nature but, rather, in hostile, 'confrontation' with it".

In any case, this verse leads us to the idea that near the Doomsday mankind by then would have gained complete mastery over their environment. Earth would have been developed into a beautiful place to live. They would have gained control over its resources and be proud of their technical marvels.

Present age may seem close toachieving this goal. To some extent they have already started controlling their environment and freely exploiting its resources. Deserts are being converted to gardens and even far off areas are being developed into places of beauty. In this regard Prophet of Allah once[44] said, 'Near the end of this world there would be so much wealth that people may not find anyone to accept charity'. He is also quoted to have said that near Doomsday even the, desert dwellers and nomads will be living in high rising buildings. Then he said, "Dajall (دجال), who will be an evil conquerer will appear near the end of the world, and would be able to travel from East to West in one single day; and will put life in the dead". All these are the signs of a high tech.civilization beginning of which seems in the rising.

Another very important aspect of high tech.developments near the doomsday is manifested in the verses 55(33-35), that before that Day, human beings on earth would have acquired the capability of deep space travel also. When they see the signs of the approaching fate on earth, urge of survival will compel them to leave it and seek refuge to other regions of the universe, but even that would not be enough to save them. This has been reminded in the following manner:—

"O' Company of Jinns and Mankind,	٣٣- يٰمَعْشَرَ الْجِنِّ وَالْإِنْسِ إِنِ اسْتَطَعْتُمْ
If Ye have the authority,	
To penetrate regions of heavens and earth,	أَنْ تَنْفُذُوا مِنْ أَقْطَارِ السَّمٰوٰتِ وَالْأَرْضِ
Then penetrate them,	فَانْفُذُوا
Ye will never penetrate them,	
Save with power,	لَا تَنْفُذُونَ إِلَّا بِسُلْطٰنٍ ۚ
Which of the favours of your Lord,	
Then ye deny?"	٣٤- فَبِأَيِّ آلَاءِ رَبِّكُمَا تُكَذِّبٰنِ ۝
.....55(33-34).	

God will thus favour mankind and the Jinns, a kind of Energy-beings, whom, by that time man might have not only known but be friended also; with the power to leave the earth and penetrate deep into space. In the following verse 55(35) we find that, even their marvellous technical ability will be of no avail. As they fly out they will encounter fatal radiations from which they would have no escape. This awful fate is predicted in the following revelation:—

"There will be sent against you both,
Heat of fire and flash of brass,
That ye will not escape"
....55(35).

۳۵- يُرْسَلُ عَلَيْكُمَا شُوَاظٌ مِّن نَّارٍ ۙ
وَّنُحَاسٌ فَلَا تَنتَصِرَانِ ○

An other reflection of the coming high tech. civilization is evident from the verse 41(53). Here, fourteen hundred years ago, Quran told that before long mankind on earth will be seeing new horizons of cosmos and on earth they will have discovered secrets of their own creation and their life. This Promise contained in the following verse is now self evident to all of us;

"Soon, We shall show them,
Our signs in the horizons,
And within themselves,
untill it becomes manifest to them,
That this (Quran) is the Truth"
...41(53).

۵۳- سَنُرِيهِمْ آيٰتِنَا فِي
الْآفَاقِ وَفِي أَنفُسِهِمْ حَتّٰى
يَتَبَيَّنَ لَهُمْ أَنَّهُ الْحَقُّ ۗ
أَوَلَمْ يَكْفِ بِرَبِّكَ
أَنَّهُ عَلٰى كُلِّ شَيْءٍ شَهِيدٌ ○

It is no wonder that as predicted by the Holy Quran fourteen centuries ago we have started witnessing the technical marvels of space age, biotechnology and medical sciences. But this is not something to rejoice. After it, future is quite clear. Doomsday cannot be far off also. Shall we not even then believe?

إِنَّ الَّذِينَ ءَامَنُوا وَالَّذِينَ هَادُوا ١٧
وَالصَّٰبِـِٔينَ وَالنَّصَٰرَىٰ وَالْمَجُوسَ
وَالَّذِينَ أَشْرَكُوا إِنَّ اللَّهَ يَفْصِلُ بَيْنَهُمْ
يَوْمَ الْقِيَٰمَةِ إِنَّ اللَّهَ عَلَىٰ كُلِّ شَيْءٍ شَهِيدٌ

Lo! Those who believe (this Revelation),
And those who are Jews,
And the Sabaeans and the Christians,
And the Magians and the Idolaters,
Lo! Allah will decide between them
On the Day of Resurrection.
Lo! Allah is witness over all things.

22(17)

Chapter-10.

PREDICTIONS ABOUT DOOMSDAY IN THE SAYINGS OF THE PROPHET OF ALLAH

Muhammad (peace be upon him) is the last of the Messengers of Allah. He told that before him, God had sent to the world over one hundred and twenty four thousands prophets in various times to various people of the world, to teach them about the purpose of life and give them awareness of their Creator. He being the last one of the prophets, signifies that the Doomsday on earth may not be too far off now. He said, "My coming is the news of the coming of the Last Hour" (Tirmizi). In the following we shall quote some of his sayings, as a further reminder of the pending Fate.

1. Hazrat Hazifah Bin Aussad, quoting the prophet of Allah narrated the following signs of the approaching doomsday. (Ref. Tirmazi, Muslim).

(a) "Dajjal (دَجّال) will appear who will be an evil ruler; enemy of the righteous everywhere and will enjoy great authority and miraculous powers. He will have means to travel from East to West in a day or part thereof. He will have with him Jannat and Jahanum. Jannat for his followers and Jahannam for his opponents. He will be able to make dead living". (From the nature of his authority, one can see that he will be master of high technology which he will use for his evil ends. Present means of high speed travel and medical developments is a step towards the coming events.)

(b) Dabt-al-Ardh (دابۃ الارض) a strange kind of creature will appear on the earth which will be an animal but speak like humans. (May be it will be also a high tech. product of bio-engineering researches which are being pursued so rigorously now).

(c) Finally there will come the event when sun will appear to rise from the West followed by some great upheaval.

(d) Near the Doomsday there will occur severe earthquakes due to which large tract of earth will sink, beginning one in the East, one in the West and one in the Arabia.

(e) Finally sky will then be overcast with smoke. Earth all over, would experience catastrophic red wind storms which may continue for years.

(f) During this period Earth will also experience excessive meteorite showers falling like stones on it.

(g) Another feature of the coming Doomsday would be that human races due to their evil deeds will gradually mutate into animal like shapes and plunge into moral bankruptcy.

If we reflect in the above predictions, world seems to be entering into this phase of Doomsday,. Rate of mutant births is gradually increasing particularly as a result of the effects of radiations. Technical developments in the field of space and biotechnology are going on as if to fulfill the predictions about Dajjal and Dabat-al-Ardh.

2. In another tradition Hazrat Abu Hurira reported that Prophet of Allah had said:—

(a) Before the Doomsday people will build high rising buildings.

(b) There will be frequent earthquakes.

(c) Time will appear moving very fast.

(d) People will be so rich that there will be no one to accept charity.

(e) There will be too much turmoil, murder and unrest, so much so that the living will prefer being dead.

(f) Then there would occur the event, that sun will rise from West instead of East, that will be the period when you should consider that Doomsday is going to approach in no time. It will be such a sudden event that a man will not have time to place in his mouth, what will be in his hand (Bukhari, Muslim).

Thinking upon the above predictions, one sees that many of these are already true. High rising buildings are being built in competition, all over the world; People are so busy that time feels like flying It is the most common complaint that they have no time. People are becoming richer and richer each day with higher living standard; but inspite of this prosperity, there is so much tension, turmoil and social disorder that no one has peace of mind. With all that coming true, perhaps we are waiting for the final event of the rising of the sun from the West·

3. Hazrat Abu Hurira narrates that Prophet of Allah had said, "Last Hour will not come, untill a fire emerges out in Hajaz, so big and intense , that necks of the camels in Basra (Iraq) will be seen during night in the light of that fire". (Bukhari, Muslim).

It is reported that such a fire came out on the 3rd of the 6th month of 654 Hijri, Near Madina.[45]

4. Hazrat Ans reported on the authority of the Prophet of Allah, "Before the Last Hour, time will become so fast that years will appear as a month; and a month as a week; and week as a day; and day as an hour and hour as a burst of fire"(Tirmizi). Does it not refer to the very busy life style of the people which we are witnessing now. Also technical developments in the field of transport has gradually shrunken distances and reduced time, firstly from months to days, then from days to hours and now from hours to minutes.

If we take this tradition in its literal meanings then it may mean the faster motion of earth around the sun or shorter orbit of the earth and also faster motion of the earth around its own axis. It is known that in its early history, a day on earth used to be as small as few hours. Gradually, as it has been slowing down, duration of the day has been also increasing accordingly. The process may reverse in the future.

5. Hazrat Anas narrated on the authority of the Prophet of Allah that signs of the Doomsday are;(Ref. Bukhari, Muslim). "Near the Doomsday knowledge (of Islam) will disappear and ignorance will prevail all over the world. Then, there will be too much adultary; wine will be consumed in large quantities. Near the Doomsday population of females will increase over males, so much so that there will be one man compared to fifty women".

In the present age we see that some of the events predicted herein are already there, particularly, in the western societies which are distinguished by heavy wine drinking and free sex practices. Unfortunately knowledge of the Quran is declining in the muslim societies also.

6. When Abdullah Bin Salam asked the prophet about the First sign of the Last Hour, he said, "First sign of the Last Hour, will be a fire that will drive the people from East toward the West".(Bukhari-Chapter Fitnah)

It should be literally true.[14] However in his commentary on this Hadith, Muhammad Asad says, "this appears to be an allegorical description of social cataclysm which will destroy the foundation of eastern cultures and will drive the people of East toward a blind imitation of the West. It is described as a 'fire' because, like fire, it will consume the remaining cultural strength of eastern people, and turn their past into dead history without connection with the present." (Page 241, English Translation and Commentary of Sahih-Al Bukhari by Mohammad Asad Pub. 1981 by Dar-Al-Audlus Gibraltar).

This account is supported from an other tradition of the Prophet of Allah, that, "muslims near the Last Hour, will follow the christian and jews blindly, so much so that, if they enter into a hole having a deadly snake in it, they will not hesitate to follow them". (Bukhari,Muslim).

7. Once Prophet of Allah said, "Before the Last Hour, Muslims will fight with Persian and win over them; they will fight with Romans and will be victorious. Decedents of the Kings of Persia and Rome will be their servants. But then they will fall into false pride, and the worst among them will be made the rulers of the last of the people. That will be the first sign of the approach of the Last Hour (Tirmizi, Muslim). On another occasion he said, Doomsday will not come over good people (Bukhari).

8. Another very distinct sign of the coming of the Doomsday told by the Prophet of Allah is that near the Doomsday, unexpected sudden deaths would be very common. He said "Near the Doomsday unaccounted murders would be common, where killer will not know his victim and the victim will not know why and who had killed him". (Bukhari).

Unfortunately we are witnessing this state of affairs also. Millions of people are dying every year suddenly through various type of accidents and sudden diseases such as the heart attacks. Then, numerous people die through the terrorist attacks, where the killers do not know their victims and likewise the people being killed through such means have not personal enmity with their killers.

9. About the muslims, Prophet of Allah said, "Near the Doomsday, they will be too many, but like the trash on the flowing water, having little weight"

A careful reflection into the predictions and signs given in the Holy Quran and told by the Holy Prophet, clarify beyond doubt that what had been said fourteen hundred years ago, we are personally witnessing some of these signs now. This high technology civilization, littered with tension, unrest, unaccounted murders, adultery and wine is inviting its own Doomsday at any time. State of Islam; that knowledge of religion will be lifted up and that the muslim, though too many in numbers, would not be of much significance on the world scene; is apparent now; and that they will imitate christian and jews blindly, is also a glaring reality. What does all that mean? Nothing but a warning to mankind, that the last Hour is not too far off now. Few **thousand** years , this way or that way, is of no significance but the End is imminent. Who will then learn lesson from this knowledge of the pending fate and save himself from the wrath of the Hereafter. We cannot change the events, but certainly has the free will to change ourselves. The Prophet of Allah had said, "Actions will be judged according to the intensions". At least we may strive to have the right intentions.

Length of the Doomsday

From the saying of the Holy Prophet (SAW) and revelation of the Holy Quran it appears that process of Doomsday would continue over a very long period of time. A direct reference to this fact is found in the Sura AL-MAARAJ, where Allah says:

"A questioner questioned concerning
the Dooms about to fall,
Upon the disbelievers, which
none can repel,
From Allah, Lord of the
Ascending stairways;"
"The Angels and the Spirit
ascend unto Him in a Day,
The measure where of is (as) fifty thousands years,
Therefore be patient with a patience
fair to see
They see (this Day) indeed as a far off (event)
But we see it Quite near,
The Day that the sky will (look like) molten copper
And the mountains will be like wool
And no friend will ask after a friend
....70(1–10)"

(١) سأل سائل بعذاب واقع
(٢) للكافرين ليس له دافع
(٣) من الله ذي المعارج
(٤) تعرج الملائكة والروح إليه في يوم كان مقداره خمسين ألف سنة
(٥) فاصبر صبرا جميلا
(٦) إنهم يرونه بعيدا
(٧) ونراه قريبا
(٨) يوم تكون السماء كالمهل
(٩) وتكون الجبال كالعهن
(١٠) ولا يسأل حميم حميما

From here we may interpret that period of Day of Doom will be extended over 50,000 years of ourreckoning. As from the signs of the Doomsday in the sayings of the Holy Prophet (SAW) one may even conclude that scene has already been set in. Many of these signs have already come true on earth and the remainders seem evident.

The Timing of the Doomsday

We have studied the predictions about the Doomsdays in the sayings of the Holy Prophet and in the revelations of the Holy Quran. The events mentioned therein are imminent and many of these predictions have already come true. There are some out of which the present world is passing through. But there remain many more signs which are yet to come. For example, appearance of Dajjal (دَجّال) or Daba-tul-Ardh (دَابتہ الاَرض), or rising of the sun from the west, etc are such things on the timings of which we cannot make any wild guess even. However. it is the most intriguing question which is being even asked since the appearance of mankind on our planet. All religions speak about it and all the Prophets of Allah, who as told by the last of them, have been over one hundred thousand years before him, gave the news of its coming. Since there would be no more prophet after Muhammad Rasool-ul-Allah, (SAW), therefore, his coming is itself the most striking news of the Doomsday. It must be now at our door steps.

We discussed earlier that Creator of Universe has hinted upon the remaining period of the approaching fate in the Holy Quran with the similitude of the period spent in the twinkling of an eye or even less than that, which we assume is relative to the total life of earth;

"And the matter of the Hour (of Doom) is,
but as twinkling of an eye,
Or it is near still,
Lo! Allah is able to do all things"
. . . .16(77).

٧٧ وَلِلَّهِ غَيْبُ السَّمَٰوَٰتِ وَالْأَرْضِ ۚ وَمَآ
أَمْرُ السَّاعَةِ إِلَّا كَلَمْحِ الْبَصَرِ أَوْ هُوَ أَقْرَبُ ۚ
إِنَّ اللَّهَ عَلَىٰ كُلِّ شَىْءٍ قَدِيرٌ

Twinkling of an eye is supposed to take about one-fifth (1/5) second of the time, which is 1/432000 of the length of 24 hour day of ours. Relative to the age of earth taken as 4.5 billion years, the remaining period in the Doomsday of earth is thus about 10,000 years.

This was one way of estimating the timing of the Doomsday. There is another Hadith of the Prophet of Allah, from which one can also make some qualitative guess. Prophet of Allah had said;

"Narrated Ibn Umar (رضی اللہ عنہ)Allah's Apostle (S.A.W.) said, "your stay in this world in comparison to the stay of the nations preceding you, is like the period between Asar (عصر) prayers and the sun set prayer (مغرب) (in comparison to a whole day). . . . . .(BUKHARI). This period is about 2 hours in 24 hours. Assuming that human beings like us are habitating this earth since 30,000 years, which is the most likely guess by the current science (Ref. W.L.Stober), Essential of Earth History (Basic) published in Prentice-Hall Inc. USA, 1966) then the period of the humanity after the last of the Apostles is about 2500 years, which means the remainder period of the life on earth is left by 1100 years approximately.

In answer to our original question, the most interesting revelation is by Dr. Khalifa Rashid (Ref: The Computer Speaks-God's Message to the world, April 1985, USA, reported by Kassim Ahmad, Malaysia in the Science and Technology in the Islamic World Vol.5 No.2 April-June 1987). Dr.Khalifa's interpretation is that left-over period is only 305 years. He has based his thesis on the following verse of the Holy Quran;

"We created not the heavens and earth, and all that is between them, save with truth (with a definite purpose), And Lo! the Hour is surely coming, So forgive, (O Muhammad) with a gracious forgiveness.	٨٥ وَمَا خَلَقْنَا ٱلسَّمَٰوَٰتِ وَٱلْأَرْضَ وَمَا بَيْنَهُمَآ إِلَّا بِٱلْحَقِّ ۗ وَإِنَّ ٱلسَّاعَةَ لَءَاتِيَةٌ ۖ فَٱصْفَحِ ٱلصَّفْحَ ٱلْجَمِيلَ
Lo! thy Lord! He is All-wise Creator.	٨٦ إِنَّ رَبَّكَ هُوَ ٱلْخَلَّٰقُ ٱلْعَلِيمُ
We have given thee seven of the Oft. repeated, and the great Quran" . . . .15(85–87).	٨٧ وَلَقَدْ ءَاتَيْنَٰكَ سَبْعًا مِّنَ ٱلْمَثَانِى وَٱلْقُرْءَانَ ٱلْعَظِيمَ

Dr.Khalifa interprets (سبعاً من المثانی) in the last verse 15(87) as the seven pairs of 14 with reference to the Muhammad (SAW) interim on this earth before the Doomsday. According to him the key is therefore the number 14, which he interprets to be the fourteen sets of Quranic initials (muqatta'at) which prefix certain Quranic chapters, which he has discovered to be intricately connected with the code 19. Adding the numerical equivalents of the fourteen sets of Quranic initials, he gets 1709 Lunary years as the period of Muhammad (S.A.W.) interim, thus giving 309 lunar years remaining to the end of humanity from 1400H, the year of the author's discovery.

All this proves that subject of the Timings of the Doomsday is highly speculative and its true knowledge is with God only. As for the belief in the Resurrection, it should not be important to know about the timing of the Doomsday, because when considered relative to eternity, hundred years or a million years, both have the same meanings. For a believer it is more than enough to know that it is coming and would be no different for the dead or alive. All will face it alike.

٦٦ وَهُوَ ٱلَّذِىٓ أَحْيَاكُمْ ثُمَّ يُمِيتُكُمْ
ثُمَّ يُحْيِيكُمْ إِنَّ ٱلْإِنسَـٰنَ لَكَفُورٌ

"And He it is,
Who gave you life,
Then He will cause you to die,
Then He will cause you torise again,
Lo! Man is varily ingrate".

22(66)

Chapter—11.

SCIENTIFIC MODE OF THE EARTHLY DOOMSDAY

Final Earthly Doomsday is but once for all, initiating with a terrible sudden blast, "One shout" which will surprise the people, taking them unaware 36(49). Thereafter the process may be completed over a long period of time. Before this 'Big Event', the Prophit of Allah also mentioned many possible smaller events of catastrophic nature,called (عذاب) on the earth. Holy Quran in its numerous verses has also mentioned of such small scale doomsdays, some of which have already occured on earth. Earthquakes, hurricanes, storms, shower of meteors, epidemics and wars etc; all serve the God's process of creation and recreation moving the world forward to its Doomsday, and simultaneously wiping out the unwanted elements of the human civilizations, as Quran says:—

"It is Allah Who creates and recreates from the very beginning,

إِنَّهُۥ هُوَ يُبْدِئُ وَيُعِيدُ ⑬

....85(13)

"So they were rightly seized by a mighty blast,
And we turned them into mouldy rubbish"
.... 23(41)

فَأَخَذَتْهُمُ ٱلصَّيْحَةُ بِٱلْحَقِّ فَجَعَلْنَٰهُمْ غُثَآءً ㊶

In this category of earthly doomsday; geo-history of earth suggests that there have been at least five mass extinctions of the living beings on this planet since last 200 million years, triggered by some extra-terrestrial causes. One theory is that every 26 millions years or so, a rain of comets bombards the earth. The impact of some large comets spew enough debris into the atmosphere to destroy the living beings and plants on earth, as a small scale glimpses of the pending event of the major doomsday.

Some theories suggest that such catastrophies are caused

Fig. 14: Life on earth has seen many global scale catasrophies. Example of the disappearance of Dinsaurs is but only one such example.

Pre-historic world of Dinosaures, which had its Doomsday through the strike of giant meteor, which filled earth with smoke and dust barring sun's light. Thus began an ice age and buzzing life was destroyed to give way to a new type of living beings. Such catastrophic, small or big events have happened frequently in the past and can happen any time now also.

by the asteroids which circle our sun, and on occasions, for unknown reasons, they crash onto earth. On smaller scale, fall of meteors from outer space have been much more frequent than the large scale catastrophies referred above.

As far the mechanism of the apparent clock-like regularity of crashes of heavenly bodies on earth, it is considered that it may be brought about by a companion star of the sun which periodically comes close enough, to pull comets or asteroids out of their natural habitat, sending them hurtling towards earth. Some theories assign this role to the slow bobbing ride of the sun on its journey in the Milky Way Galaxy, which is an island of 100 billion stars, shaped something like a stunny-side-up egg, 100,000 light years in diameter, with a bulge (the yolk) in the middle and three flat, dusty arms (the egg white) forming a circle around it. Like all its fellow stars, the sun revolves around the galactic centre, taking about 250 million years to complete a round trip. As it moves, it bobs up and down, through the central plane of the galaxy, where most of the stars and dust clouds are concentrated. In this hazardous journey, possibility of a crash is always there, which may happen any time, initiating the act of the major doomsday of the earth or of the solar system as a whole.

Evidence in favour of an impact is thus rapidly accumulating. Scientific discoveries tend to conclude, if comets do strike in barrages every 26 million years from now, we are in for some trouble. But it is also possible, even probable, that long before that time, astronomers will spot a random, incoming comet or asteroid nudged by the gravity of an outer planet or star, into a direct collision course with the earth, bringing its doomsday suddenly.

Referring back to the Quranic verse 36(49) i.e. "They wait not but one blast, which will surprise them while they are disputing", the impact theory given above seems to be progressing in the right direction.

SCIENTIFIC VIEW OF THE DOOMSDAYOF EARTH

In the scientific view Doomsday of the earth is closely connected with the life of the Sun.[37,10] Paul Davies, has reviewed the scientific findings on this subject and presented the scenario of this awful event as follows:—

"As far as our local region of the universe is concerned the fate of the Earth is intimately linked with the fate of the sun. Earth life feeds on sunlight, and any major disruption to the sun's present quiescence will spell disaster. There is no lack of possible solar twitches that could render the earth uninhabitable. Any alteration in the sun's constant heat output could upset the Earth's delicate climatic balance and plunge us into a catastrophic ice age. Changes in the magnetic patterns of the solar system connected with the so-called solar wind i.e. steady stream of particles from the sun's surface might bring about equally drastic changes. The explosion of a nearby star could trench us in lethal radiation, or the passage of a black hole through the solar system might rock the planets in their orbits".

But assuming the Earth escapes all these unpleasant possibilities it is clear that things cannot continue as now "for ever and ever". The prolific radiation of energy by the sun has to be paid for in nuclear fuel, and eventually the fuel reserves will start to runout. Astrophysicists estimate[37] that this will not happen for another four to five billion years, which may seem a large length of time. However, by comparison to the age of eighteen billion years of the universe, it is a little period.

As the fuel runs low, so the sun will swell up, turning into the sort of star that astronomers call a red giant. Gradually it will become big enough to engulf the inner planets; then the Earth's atmosphere will be stripped away and the solid rocks melted or even vaporized.

Thereafter, the sun will embark on a new and erratic career, in which the nuclear burning of hydrogen fuel, so prolific today, will be replaced by the less efficient burning of helium, and thence by heavier and heavier elements. When finally all fuel is exhausted, the sun will consist of moderately heavy elements such as iron. Any further fusion of nuclei would not result in the release of energy. Iron is the most stable nuclear form, and according to the second law of thermodynamics, all systems seek out their most stable state. During this phase the sun's central temperature will

Fig.15. Life cycle of the sun, if all goes well and it is allowed to grow old undisturbed, it will end as a black dwarf. Earth will be destroyed much earlier.

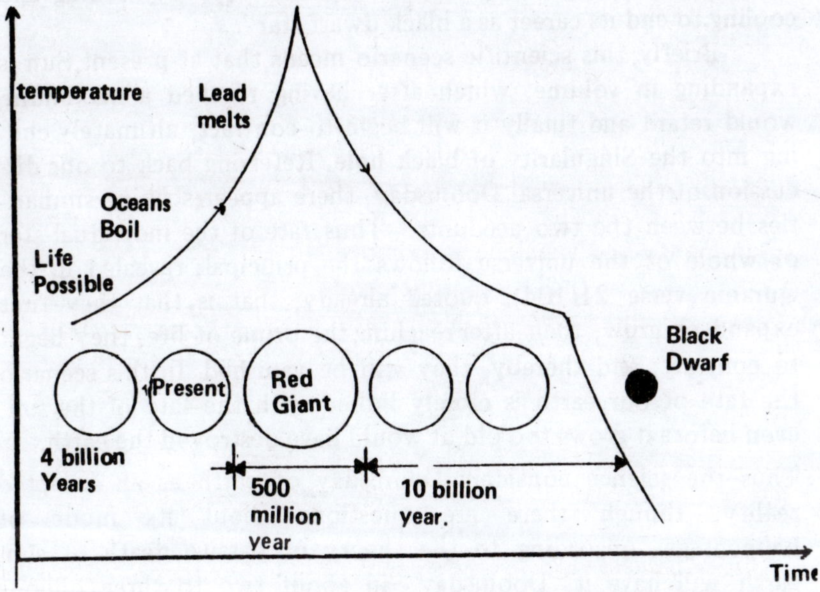

The sun is now a middle aged star, it is gradually expanding. It will continue to brighten moderately for another 5 billion years. Thereafter the sun will consume its hydrogen rapidly and swell in size accordingly. Temperature on earth will rise so much so that water in the ocean will boil, lead will melt on the earth. Then the sun will begin to cool and shrink. Temperature on earth will reduce to freezing point. Sun will end as a black dwarf in the sky.

Above is the likely story, if the sun is allowed to grow old comfortably. However chances of accident are quite high in the space. In that case sun along with its family members may die even younger.

have risen steadily towards a billion degrees. Now, with all fuel spent, the internal pressure will fall and gravity will take command. The aged sun will start to contract under its own weight, crushing the material within it so violently that the density will rise to a million grams per cubic centimetre, slowly fading and cooling,to end its career as a black dwarf star".

Briefly, this scientific scenario means that at present Sun is expanding in volume, which after having reached a maximum, would retard and finally it will begin to contract, ultimately ending into the Singularity of black hole. Referring back to our discussion of the universal Doomsday, there appears striking similarities between the two accounts. Thus fate of the individual star or whole of the universe follows the principal; revealed in the Quranic verse 21(104), quoted already, that is, that they first expand or grow, then after reaching the prime of life, they begin to contract; and thereby, they will be vanished. In this scenario the fate of our earth is closely linked with the fate of the sun. even before it grows too old, it would have destroyed the earth.

Thus the science considers Doomsday of earth as an accepted reality, though there are questions about its mode of happenings. According to the theory of passive death of sun, earth will have its Doomsday in about two to three billions years. But if we take into account the possibility of a crash or an accident in the heavens which science does not over-rule, it may come any time.

Chapter—12

MECHANICS OF THE EARTHLY DOOMSDAY

There are a number of verses in the Holy Quran which describe vividly the events of the Earthly Doomsday. From these verses, a scientific mind may work backwards and analyse their mechanism of occurrence. Some of the major events, with their possible causes are discussed below. It must, however be realized that mechanism given herein are based upon scientific reasoning and therefore subject to improvement. Earlier, we have discussed that Holy Quran speaks about the start up of the earthly Doomsday in some sudden way. In the verses 69(13-15), it has been said to occur with a terriblly intense sound, referred in Arabic as Soor (صور). A careful analysis of the various verses of the Holy Quran on this subject leads one to the following three mechanisms of the earthly Doomsday:—

(a) A GREAT CRASH: According to it earthly Doomsday may initiate by the fall of some outer space body such as a giant meteor, impact of which would push earth out of its orbit, and subsequently with each cycle brings it closer to the Sun and finally destroyed by falling into the Sun. This would lead to a gradual upheavel of the solar system to its destruction also.

(b) A GREAT EXPLOSION: This represents a much more dramatic end of the earth, which inside its body contains molten lava under very high pressures, and may explode like a bomb; thus destroying itself suddenly. This theory is backed up by the general principle of Doomsday derived from the verse 21(104); which is that universe would see its End when its present mode of expansion changes into contraction, and then on reaching certain critical volume it will explode back. On this principle, earth which has been in the contracting phase[38] since long would explode like a super-pressure vessel in the end.

(c) Most probably both the impact mechanism and the explosion mechanism are part of the earthly doomsday and will occur at separate intervals; that is, the great crash marks the start up of the Doomsday and the explosion may complete it. In the following we shall discuss these issues in greater details, with specific reference to the information gathered from the Holy Quran and the current scientific findings.

Fig.16: Some Possible Modes of the Destruction of Earth:

16.1: Earth has been contracting in size since its inception. In tne beginning it was probably 100 times its present size. As the earth contracts, internal pressure in its core is also rises A stage may reach when it can no longerhold that pressure, and may explode like a pressure vessel.

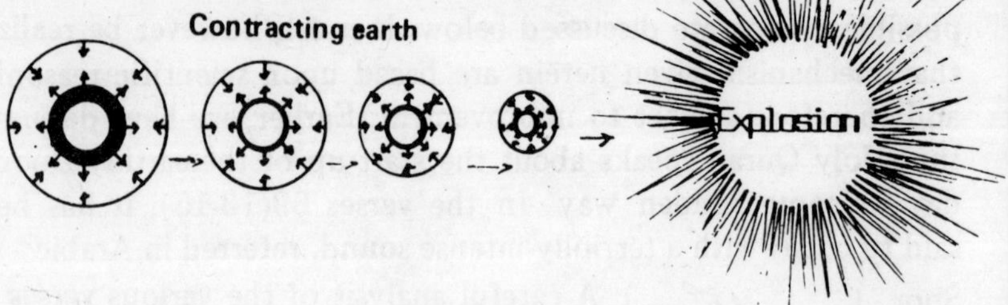

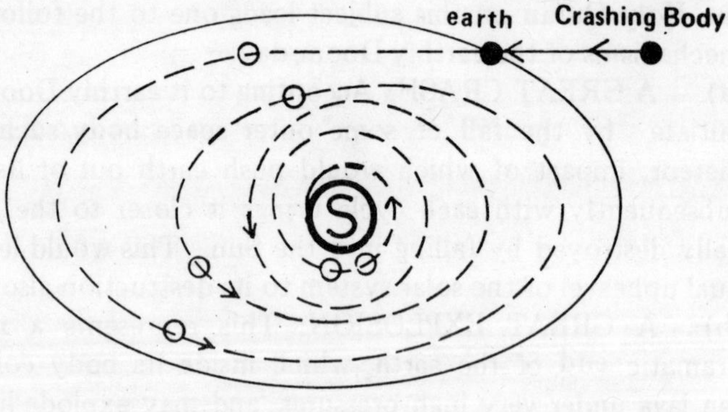

16:2 Crash of some heavenly body, say a giant meteor may push earth out of its present orbit toward the sun. Then in each revolution it would get nearer to the sun. When being too near, ultimately it may loose its moon. Latter approach will fill it with hot solar smoke. Internally, the higher gravity of sun will effect the molten matter in the core of earth, causing convulsions in its interior, excessive earth quakes and volcanic activity. Ultimately earth may explode and destroy itself, falling into sun and annihilated. If the crash puts earth, say 0.1 degree off its present track toward the sun, then at its present speed of rotation of 19 miles per second or 67,000 miles per hours, it can fall into the sun in a period of about 100 years. But life on earth may be roasted about 40 years after the crash. With the closing radious the perpherial velocity of earth will also increase. This will result in greater centrifugal forces on it, resulting into breaking of mountains and continuous earthquakes.

CONTRACTION OF EARTH

On the subject of gradual evolution of Earth, Holy Quran gives us the revolutionary concept, that it is contracting from all sides. The process may have been continuing ever since its inception. This is seen from the following verse; addressed particularly to those who have come to know of this great secret of nature but to their misfortune, do not believe in the God, Who causes it and had revealed this fact, fourteen hundreds years ago for their guidance:—

"See they not?
How We are,
Reducing the Earth gradually,
From its all sides"
....13(41)

﴿٤١﴾ أَوَلَمْ يَرَوْا أَنَّا نَأْتِي الْأَرْضَ نَنقُصُهَا مِنْ أَطْرَافِهَا

The earlier commentators of the Holy Quran had interpreted the words; "Reducing of Earth" (نَنقُصُهَا) as the spread of Islam over the globe. There is no reason to deny this interpretation also. However, since the Holy Quran is the word of God having no ambiguities, literal meanings of its verses must also be true. Thus, the verse 13(41) points out towards a phenomena of great geological importance which is that, "Earth has been gradually shrinking in size from all directions and the process continues.

This will mean that originally Earth must have been of much bigger size. Latest scientific theories on its evolution also conform to this astonishing revelation. According to them, in the beginning, Earth was at least 100 times bigger in volume and has shrunk to its present size over the last five billion years of its existence.[38]

There are several ways to explain the shrinkage of Earth. Force of gravity seems to have played the principal role in this phenomena. A concurrent cause is thought to be the escape of volatile matter from the earth, which has been vapouring to space due to the solar heat falling on its surface and radioactive heat generated within its body. A small contribution to the shrinkage can also be associated with the gradual cooling effect, which would mean that crust has been increasing in thickness with simultaneous reduction in the size of the molten core.

Whatever the reasons of this strange phenomena, fact remains that earth is shrinking in size. However, one is struck by the tone of the verse 13(41), which seems to hint upon that this phenomena must be of some extraordinary importance for mankind.

EXPLOSION:

The most important implication of the contraction of earth might be that it is moving towards its self destruction. With the contraction, pressure on the internal molten mass should also increase. A stage could reach when further increase of pressure should react back in the form of violent explosion of its core, like failure of a super boiler. In this case, it would automatically initiate other events of the Doomsday, such as violent earthquakes, smoke in the atmosphere, boiling of oceans, flying of mountains, etc: to be discussed later in this paper.

GREAT CRASH:

An alternative mechanism of the initiation of Doomsday as discussed already is by the impact of some external heavenly body falling on earth. Verses 69(13-15) directly hint upon such possibility. Itcouldbe a blast with an explosive noise, which will sound the beginning of Doomsday. Revelation is:—

فَإِذَا نُفِخَ فِي ٱلصُّورِ نَفۡخَةٌ وَٰحِدَةٌ ﴿١٣﴾
وَحُمِلَتِ ٱلۡأَرۡضُ وَٱلۡجِبَالُ فَدُكَّتَا دَكَّةً وَٰحِدَةً ﴿١٤﴾
فَيَوۡمَئِذٍ وَقَعَتِ ٱلۡوَاقِعَةُ ﴿١٥﴾

"And when the Soor shall sound,
One blast,
Earth with the mountains,
Will be lifted up
and crushed with one crash,
Then on that Day,
The Event will fall"
....69(13-15)

EARTH WILL BE PUSHED OUT OF ITS ORBIT:

Scene of the crash depicted in the verses 69(13-15) indicates that it should be due to some extra-terrestrial mechanism, may be some giant asteroid or some other heavenly object of large mass, which will strike and lift earth out from its present position in the solar system. Nature of this impact might be such that it pushes the earth toward the sun, which means that gravitational pull of sun will increase on it. New orbit of earth would be then like the gradual winding up of a spiral disc, which will move it closer to sun in each revolution as shown in Fig. 16.

Strike by a giant asteroid on earth is an open probability in science of today also. According to Nigel Henbest[10] earth may be harmed by the fall of large meteorites. Such cosmic catastrophe have been widely discussed recently (see for example D.Clark, G. Hunt & W. Mirea, New Scientist Vol. 80 pp 861, 1978), though of much smaller magnitude, it is thought that the extinction of dinosaurs and many other species simultaneously in the past, was caused by a 10 KM diameter astroid hiting the Earth 65 million years ago, (Reported in New Scientist Vol. 85. P.59, 1980). To eliminate life on Earth entirely, it would require a catastrophic order of magnitude worse. Asteroids ten times larger than the one thought to have destroyed the dinosaurs may do the job. Moreover, solar system is thought to be so sensitive to external happenings that even if a Supernova explodes at a distance of 10 light years away from earth, it would seriously effect its stability and life.

Faster Motion of Earth:

After the crash, as the orbit of the earth around the sun shrinks, its orbital velocity will increase inversely proportional to its distance from the centre of sun. This could also result into the increase of the velocity of earth around its own axis. Enhancement of velocities will result into the enhancement of the centrifugal forces acting on the body of earth. Consequently, the matter from the earth such as mountains will separate and thrown into space. Also the water in the oceans will gush out into the space. The internal molten lava in the core will also be subjected to increased cyclic pressures, which may ultimately result into the bursting open of the earth. Moreover the time period of the year and the day would decrease gradually, fulfilling the prophecy of the Prophet of Allah, that near the Doomsday, year will be as the month, month as if the week, the week as if the day and the day as if the hour. (Bukhari - Muslim).

قال رب انصرني بما كذبون ٣٩

قال عما قليل ليصبحن نادمين ٤٠

فأخذتهم الصيحة بالحق فجعلناهم غثاء ٤١
فبعدا للقوم الظالمين

ثم أنشأنا من بعدهم قرونا آخرين ٤٢

ما تسبق من أمة أجلها وما يستأخرون ٤٣

"The(Prophet)said,My Lord!
Help me because they deny me.
He(God)said,in a little while
they will become repentent,
So the(awful)cry overtook them rightfully,
And we made them like as wreckage,
A far removal for wrong doing folk
Then after them We brought
forth other generations,
No nation can outstrip its term,
Nor yet postpone it"

23(39-43)

Chapter—13.

SOME GREAT EVENTS OF THE EARTHLY DOOMSDAY WITH CAUSES

Based upon our understanding of the Quranic revelations, in the following we shall discuss some of the great events of the earthly Doomsday, which could be of special significance to the scientists in their understanding of this reality in real terms. An effort has also been made to assign causes to such events, which should be helpful to those who may like to pursue this subject for further research:

(i) *High Temperature on Earth.*

There are some verses in the Holy Quran which indicate that during doomsday, temperature on earth will rise, so much so, that water in the oceans will begin to boil:—

"(Consider the events),
When the oceans
Boil over"
. . . .81(6)

وَإِذَا ٱلْبِحَارُ سُجِّرَتْ ⑥

This can be explained to happen in several ways. One possibility could be due to the earth having been brought closer to sun as visualised by the impact theory. Under the combined effects of higher velocity, temperature and gravitational pull, earth would begin to loose its atmosphere and water in the oceans will then begin to boil. However, a more likely reason of the boiling of oceans may be in the explosion theory due to the release of internal heat of earth. On a smaller scale, it may also be attributed to the excessive volcanic activity which, as we shall discuss later, are going to be too frequent near the Doomsday. We already know that, though on a limited scale, boiling of sea water due to the under-sea volcanic activity is a well observed phenomena even now. Another possibility of the rise of temperature on earth to the boiling point of water is that sun expands and thus comes nearer to the earth. According to the current scientific thought it is very much likely to happen with the aging of the sun after Five to Six billion years in the future. Thus we see that boiling of oceans can happen through many ways; one or some of these mechanisms together, can cause this event near the Doomsday.

(ii) *Oceans on Fire*

Revelation 82(3), leads us to the idea that during Earthly Doomsday, something dramatic will occur which would put oceans on fire. It says:—

"(Consider) when the oceans would Burst on fire, — ٣ وَإِذَا الْبِحَارُ فُجِّرَتْ

And when the graves are overturned" — ٤ وَإِذَا الْقُبُورُ بُعْثِرَتْ

. . . .82(3-4)

One can easily say that the cause of the fire in the oceans must be due to other than the simple effects of higher solar energy received by the earth near the Doomsday. The connected phrase, in the verse 82(4), "When the graves are overturned". invites our attention to the idea that this might occur due to the bursting of the earth's interior, which is easily explainable by the explosion theory discussed already. To a lesser degree, same could be possible by the violent release of red hot lava by the under-sea burst of volcanoes, which has been noticed to give the impression of the ocean on fire.

(iii) *Hydrocarbon in the Interior of Earth.*

Knowing that water cannot catch fire easily, we may draw a very important corollary from the verses 82(3-4), that interior of earth might contain large amount of hydrocarbons, like methane, which on leaking out from the beds of seas, would catch fire and produce the effect of oceans on fire. Same is possible through the spill of under-sea petroleum reservoirs also, which might be caused by the break of earth's crust under the seas through violent earthquakes during its Doomsday.

(iv) *Earth's Atmosphere filled with Smoke*

Holy Quran, in its verses 44(10-11), points out that one special feature of Doomsday would be the appearance of large amount of smoky matter in the atmosphere of earth. Divine Revelation is:—

"Watch for the Day,
When the heaven will bring forth,
A kind of smoke,
Plainly visible,
Enveloping people,
This will be painfully
grievous"
.44(10-11)

١٠ فَارْتَقِبْ يَوْمَ تَأْتِي السَّمَاءُ بِدُخَانٍ مُّبِينٍ

١١ يَغْشَى النَّاسَ هَٰذَا عَذَابٌ أَلِيمٌ

There can be various possibilities for this happening too. The simplest explanation could be through excessive volcanic action. In fact, history has recorded the overcasting of sky for months due to the dust released in the explosion of the huge volcanoes in the past also.[24] So much so that it had prevented the sunlight reaching earth, making its winters too severe for all types of life on it. The explosion theory suggests that atmosphere could be overcast with the smoke released from the inner core of the earth.

But, overcasting of skies with smoke could also be possible due to the crash of huge meteorites from outside as discussed already in the case of impact theory. The same might also be possible due to some explosion in a nearby planet or in the sun itself which can fill the space with plasma of hot gaseous matter. In fact scientific evidence suggests that killing of Dinosaurs, some sixty millions years ago, was brought by the overcasting of the earth's atmosphere by dust, caused by the impact of some 10 KM dia astroid on earth, which released so much debris that sun light was prevented reaching it for years. This had caused very low temperatures and darkness, consequently all life was killed in a matter of few years only.[24,7]

Noting that in the verses 44(10-11), smoke has been said to be overcasting earth from heaven, most probable mechanism of this may be attributed to the large scale disturbances in the sun itself. In this regard, science of astronomy is already familiar with the solar flares which occasionally shoot out from the sun upto distances of hundreds of thousands miles, scattering hot plasma

Fig. 17 Outburst from the Sun

A prominence rising over 150,000 km above the photosphere. (Courtesy Mt. Wilson Observatory, Carnegie Institution of Washington)

The verses 44(10-11) point out that near the time of its doomsday, earth will be overcast by smoke, which will fill the space alaround. The Figure shows the photograph of the solar flares which explode out occasionally and throw the solar matter in space. These hot burst of solar gases emerge explosively and rise to considerable heights. Normal prominances rise over a million miles from the surface of the Sun at speed of 450 miles per second. The passage of the intense streams of radiation and particles through the solar system are of great concern to those responsible for manned space flights. During severe solar activity the dosages, even at the distances of the earth, are extremely high . From the Holy Quran, it is derived that the period of the earthly Doomsday might be a period of very intense solar activity also. Perhaps at that time storms in the sun may burst out very hot plasma gases as far as our earth.

into .space. Figure .17 shows one such representation. If some-how it happens on a much larger scale then it could reach the earth also. However, considering enormous distance separating these two it should take atleast 20 to 30 years before smoke actually could reach the earth. This mechanism appears to be supported by the verses 75(7—11) given below also:—

"The sight is confounded,
And the moon is buried in darkness,
And the sun and moon,
They are joined together:
On that day,
Man will cry,
Whither to flee?
Alas, no refuge"
....75(7-11)

٧ فَإِذَا بَرِقَ الْبَصَرُ
٨ وَخَسَفَ الْقَمَرُ
٩ وَجُمِعَ الشَّمْسُ وَالْقَمَرُ
١٠ يَقُولُ الْإِنسَانُ يَوْمَئِذٍ أَيْنَ الْمَفَرُّ
١١ كَلَّا لَا وَزَرَ

These verses have pointed out a number of events of the Doomsday which need careful analysis. For example, confounding of the sight might be due to the bright flash of huge solar flares produced at the start-up of the event which would subsequently overcast the earth with smoke. Burying of moon in darkness should be after space has been littered with the smoky stuff preventing the sun-light reaching it. This would then lead to the gradual overcasting of the earthly atmosphere with poisonous solar smoke, causing suffocation. This terrible state of affairs is reflected by the last part of the revelation; that mankind cry in the state of utter helplessness, "where to flee", and there is no refuge.

(v) *Rising of the Sun From West*

As narrated earlier, in one of his traditions, the Holy Prophet is reported to have said that, at the outset of the Doomsday, Sun will appear to the inhabitants of the world rising from the west against its normal appearance in the east. The impact theory can explain this abnormal happening because the severity and the direction of the strike can change the motion of the earth on its own axis also. Reversal of this motion can result into rising of the sun from the west everywhere.

Since the sudden phenomenon of the sun rising from the west is difficult to be explained by any other mean than the reversal of the motion of earth around its own axis, this hadith of the prophet of Allah, thus directly lends its support to the impact theory also.

(vi) *Earthquakes and Great Commotion*

One of the most obvious features of the earthly Doomsday understood from the Holy Quran and from the sayings of the Holy Prophet is that during this phase, earth would experience terrible earthquakes, utmost convulsions and severe vibrations, breaking its crust apart, structures destroyed, mountains uprooted, volcanoes brusting with the internal molten lava gushing out everywhere. This terrible scene is visualized from the following verses:—

"When earth,
Is shaken again and again,
To her utmost convulsions,
And it throws up,
Her burden from within"
. . . .99(1-2)

١ إِذَا زُلْزِلَتِ الْأَرْضُ زِلْزَالَهَا

٢ وَأَخْرَجَتِ الْأَرْضُ أَثْقَالَهَا

Earth being shaken again and again is understood to mean a continuous series of earthquakes of severe magnitude, which according to the adjoining verse 99(2), i.e. "earth throws up its burden from within" would break apart its crust.Current scientific knowledge is that even the earthquakes of intensity of about 8 on Richter scale are highly disastrous for all types of man-made structures. At 9 and over, earth's crust opens up with the breaking of mountains and disappearance of rivers. This can trigger large scale volcanic activity also. With the repeated earthquakes of intensity over 9, earth would be levelled off, with everything upside down.

A deeper look into the verses given below reflect that the state of earth during its Doomsday is going to be much more severe than what could be caused by the simple action of earthquakes. It is being said:—

"On That Day
everything that
can be in commotion will
be in commotion,
Followed by oft-repeated
commotion"
.79(6–7)

٦ يَوْمَ تَرْجُفُ الرَّاجِفَةُ

٧ تَتْبَعُهَا الرَّادِفَةُ

Fig.18 Earthquakes are the natures great tool of change and destruction. They break apart land masses, cause large areas to sink and rise. For example the earthquake of March 27, 1964 in Alaska caused an area of approximately 30,000 square miles to sink as 6 feed and an adjacent area of 50,000 square miles was elevated in places as much an 35 ft. Earthquakes have killed millions of people in matter of seconds. In the picture is shown the earthquakes that rocked Newsealand recently. Though only 6.5 on Richter scaie, it ripped apart the roads, destroyed many buildings. Earthquakes greater than 8.5 on Richter scale may level even the most massive man-made structures and break the mountains. They are also the nature's reminder of the small scale doomsday. Near the earthly doomsday, there will be too many high intensity earthquakes occuring all the time; shaking the earth to its depeths.

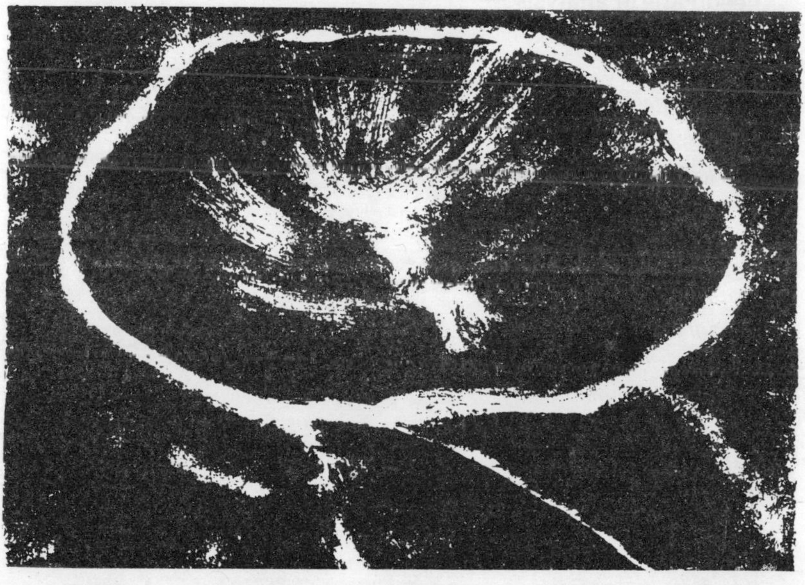

Fig.19 A metor can hit the earth and break it apart. Its force of impact can shake the earth and if, of too much intensity, could throw it out of its orbit. It may even change its direction of rotation around its axis.

Further to that,

"The earth will be ground to atoms,
pounded over pounded"
. . . .89(21)

٢١ كَلَّآ إِذَا دُكَّتِ ٱلْأَرْضُ دَكًّا دَكًّا

This scene looks like that of a ball mill used in the crushing of rocks. It is a state of terrible shake up, vibration and disorder within the body of the earth. Not only that, it would also be pounded by the crashing heavenly objects, probably by the continuous showers of meteors from outside. Internally, earth would be breaking apart by the explosions within, a situation which will be worsened by the crashes from outer space.

(vii). *Mountains Turning into Sand.*

A dramatic feature of the Doomsday is that, during that phase, all high grounds, hills, mountains and valleys on the surface of the earth will be levelled off, leaving little irregularities, mountains turning into dust, flying all around. Earth will then be nothing but a barren mound. On this, the following verses need careful analysis:—

"They ask thee concerning
the mountains,
Say, My Lord will break them,
and scatter them as dust,
He will render (earth)
Plain, smooth and level,
Nothing crooked
Will thou see in their place"
. . . 20(105–107)

١٠٥ وَيَسْـَٔلُونَكَ عَنِ ٱلْجِبَالِ فَقُلْ يَنسِفُهَا
رَبِّى نَسْفًا
١٠٦ فَيَذَرُهَا قَاعًا صَفْصَفًا
١٠٧ لَّا تَرَىٰ فِيهَا عِوَجًا وَلَآ أَمْتًا

"Thou see the mountains,
And think them firmly fixed,
But they shall pass away,
As the clouds pass away"
. . . .27(88);

٨٨ وَتَرَى ٱلْجِبَالَ تَحْسَبُهَا جَامِدَةً وَهِىَ تَمُرُّ مَرَّ
ٱلسَّحَابِ

"And the mountains,
They will become like
carded wool"
. . . .101(5)

٥ وَتَكُونُ ٱلْجِبَالُ
كَٱلْعِهْنِ ٱلْمَنفُوشِ

٤ إِذَا رُجَّتِ الْأَرْضُ رَجًّا

٥ وَبُسَّتِ الْجِبَالُ بَسًّا

٦ فَكَانَتْ هَبَاءً مُّنبَثًّا

(Consider of the Day)
"When the earth shall be shaken
to its depth,
And the mountains shall be
crumbled to atoms,
Becoming dust scattered abroad"
. . . .56(4–6)

How is all this going to happen? Under ordinary circumstances, we are aware of the slow crumbling process of rocks. Nature's agents, such as wind, rain, plants, temperature variations and chemical reactions, all help in breaking the rocks. Sand and silt in the rivers and canals is actually part of the crumbling mountains. But the destructive scenario depicted by the above quoted verses is much more dramatic than the ordinary decay processes.

One possible mechanism could be due to the already referred repeatedly occuring earthquakes during the periods of Doomsday. Quran has also said that mountains are the means of stabilizing earth against its inherent vibrations. Therefore, destruction of the mountains could provide a positive feed back effect, resulting into greater shake up of earth and its breakage.

It has also been discovered that if intensity and frequency of vibration increases above a certain thresh-hold level, solids begin to crumble and disintegrate. Therefore the commotion referred in the verses 79(6–7) may become the cause to render mountains as dust.

However, the phenomenon of shooting up of the mountains, or their becoming like the carded wool flying allround, cannot be explained by the hypothesis of vibrations alone.
It is likely to happen due to the increased centifugal forces on the body of earth. With its increasing speed of rotation around its own axis and on its orbit, as discussed already, will be thrown around like the projectiles from a potter's wheel.

Phenomena of extreme earthquakes, vibration and grinding of the earth masses,explosive release of energy and flying of mountain pieces, can also be explained by the hypothesis of exploding of the internal core of the earth. It is known that interior of the earth is under extremely high pressures, which rests in delicate equilibrium. In this respect it is like a super high pressure vessel. If per chance, it fails, the earth could explode like a bomb, with tremendous release of energy, combined with extreme degree of vibrations, high pressure waves, shake ups and explosive flying of the earth's crust and mountains. Thus there are various possible ways, which any, or all together, may cause the destructive scene revealed by the verses quoted in this chapter.

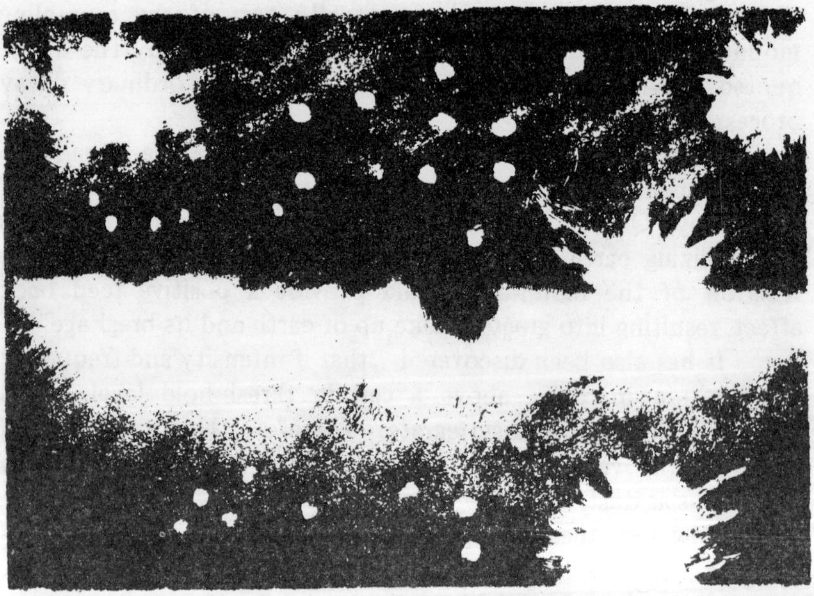

Fig.20:

Volcanoes are the sudden dramatic and catastrophic eruptions of molten lava, smoke and fire from underneath the crust of earth. When they occur in the populated areas, they cause huge damage to life and materials. In AD 79 the volcano, we now know as Vesuvius became active and destroyed the populous cities of Pompeii and Hercilamam of Italy, the former under rain of ashes and dust, the latter under a flood of mud derived from the heavy volcanoic rains. We may call it a small scale Doomsday for the inhabitants of those cities. Near its Doomsday, earth will experience too many of the volcanic eruptions also.

Chapter-14

FATE OF THE MOON

(i) *Catching of Moon by Sun.*

A very special event of the **Earthly** Doomsday is that during this period, moon leaving the earth, would join the Sun. In this regard revelation 75(8-9) is highly thought provoking:—

"The moon is buried in darkness, ⑧ وَخَسَفَ الْقَمَرُ
And the Sun and the Moon ⑨ وَجُمِعَ الشَّمْسُ وَالْقَمَرُ
are joined together"
....75(8–9)

There can be several reasons forthesephenomena also. The simplest explanation would be the overcasting of the moon by the burst of solar flares discussed already. Another plausible reason, could be due to the earth coming too close to the sun, which is explainable through the great crash theory. After the impact, earth would gradually slip away from its present orbit and adopting a spiral course, in each revolution will get closer to the sun. A stage should reach when due to its higher field of gravity, sun will snatch the earth's moon. In this connection, we already know that the planets mercury and venus, which are nearer to Sun have no moons.

If we relate this event to the linear-death-theory of the solar system, then scientifically it is known that slowly, Sun is expanding and for this reason in the next few billion years, it will swell enough in volume to swallow both the moon and earth.

(ii) *Breaking of Moon into Pieces.*

Another significant event of the solar system Doomsday revealed in the Holy Quran in its verse 54(1), is that during this period moon will split into pieces:—

"Hour of the Judgement draws near, ① اقْتَرَبَتِ السَّاعَةُ وَانْشَقَّ الْقَمَرُ
And the moon,
It will be split asunder"
....54(1)

Several reasons can be assigned to this happening also. For example, it could be said to happen due to the strike of some large meteor from outside which breaks its crust. However, it is more likely that it might happen due to some explosion in its core say, a violent moonquake. It can break apart the moon into two or more pieces, which of course can rejoin, because the verse does not speak of the moon permanently split asunder.

Fig.21: Moon is drifting away ultimately it may fall in the Sun.

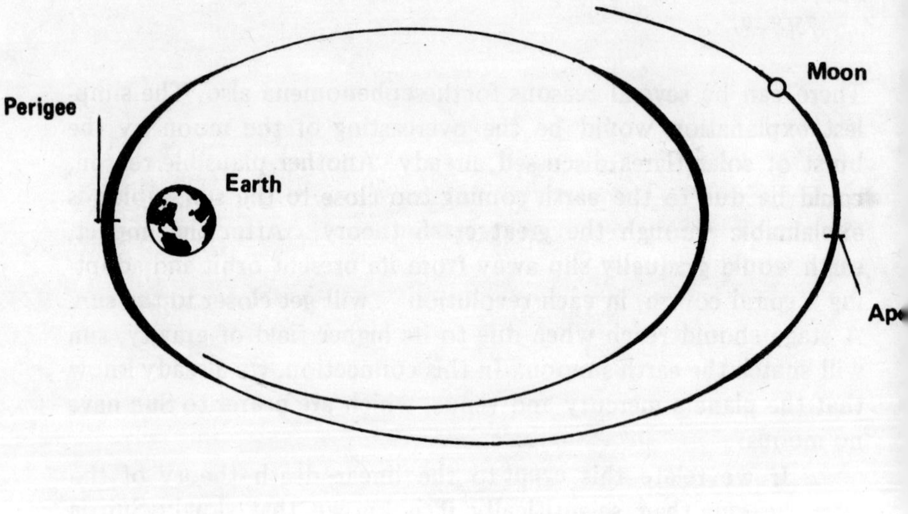

Moon is our closest neighbour some 384,000 Kilometer away. A thing of beauty which regulates the sea tides thus helping the marine life for us. It is lifeless but sometimes volcanoes also erupt on it. The moon is also bombarded by meteorites that have covered it with dust and pourus glassy matter. Moon is an alien to earth. The lattest ‹ capture › hypothesis (1955) suggests that moon was born somewhere at distant from earth in the solar system, and by chance it came nearer to the earth, and then caught by it. It was captured 5 billion years ago and came closest to the earth 1.2 billion years ago. At that time it was just 180,000 Km from earth whereas now it is 384,000 Km away from us. Since then the tidal forces kep the moon drifting away from earth. Its orbit is now becoming larger at the rate of 3 cm a year. Eventually, earth will not be able to hold the moon, and then it may fall in the sun. Linearly, it may happen in about 5 billion years from now but due to some external causes same can occur much earlier. The phenomena of moon joining the sun was predicted by the verses 75(8-9) many centuries earlier than the scientific reasoning of today.

Chapter-15.

DOOMSDAY AND SOLAR SYSTEM

As discussed already Doomsday of the Sun, is supposed to be a separate event from the earthly Doomsday. In this respect one of the most significant happening seen through the Holy Quran is that sun will drift away from its present position in the galaxy, where it has been found to have a fixed orbit, and completes one cycle in about 250 million years. Fig.13,22 show the motion of the "Sun in Space". It should be worthwhile to note that a few centuries ago people used to think of the sun as a stationary subject in the heaven. Even Coupernicus had built his revolutionary theory of revolving earth on the assumption of the fixed sun, which men of science believed true for more than two centuries; not knowing that twelve centuries before Coupernicus, Holy Quran had clearly told about the continuous travel of sun in space in its following revelation:—

"And the Sun
Keeps on rushing (in space)
On a set path,
According to some pre-fixed
measurement of the Most Powerful"
.....36(37).

٣٨ وَالشَّمْسُ تَجْرِي لِمُسْتَقَرٍّ لَهَا ذَٰلِكَ تَقْدِيرُ
الْعَزِيزِ الْعَلِيمِ

In this journey, sun passes through various regions of space. Fig.13 shows the complexity of this motion. According to the latest finding in astrophysics, reported by James Gleik[3] the galaxies with billions of stars within them, move in space like a vast celestial convoy, in which each component is a multi-discipline system of motions. For example, if our earth is revolving around the sun at a speed of 19 miles per second, to complete one revolution in one year, the Sun is streaming in the galaxy at about 200 miles per second; whereas galaxy is rushing out at more than 600 miles per second speed. All other stars have similarly multimotion system of their own. In the areas of concentration of stary worlds, the situation might be much more complex than this simple picture of mob race. Chances of inter-collisions cannot be ruled out. Near its Doomsday, Holy Quran says, something sudden will happen which will overthrow sun out of its normal

Fig.22: Journey of the Sun in Space.

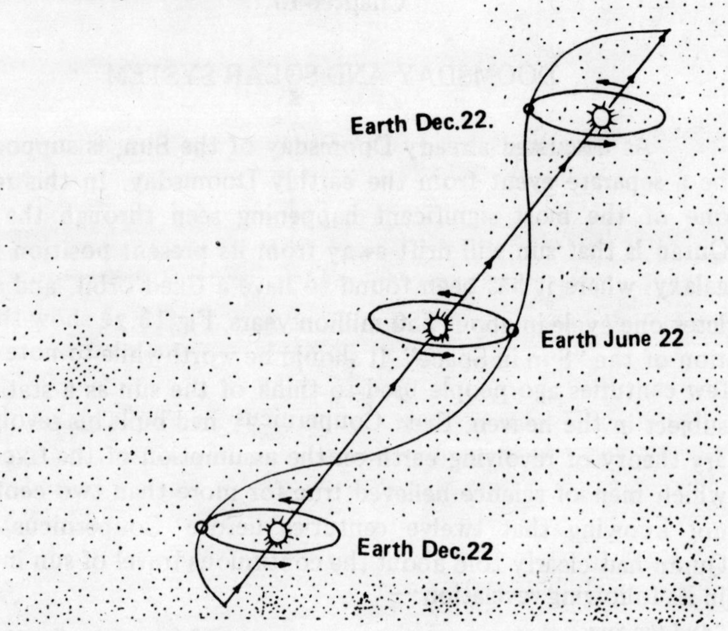

The sun keeps on rushing in space to some predestined destiny 36(38); at a speed of about 200 miles per second, 6.3x10^{9} miles a year, 66 times the distance from the earth to the Sun. Not much is known about the nature of this motion. Is it really a straight line, or are we swinging around in some supper orbit, the centre of which not yet is known? An way this is a hazardous journey in the heavens which houses as many as over a billion galaxies and millions of trillions of stars, planets and other type of heavenly bodies, possibility of crach cannot be ruled out. (Ref.Page and Page. The origin of solar system, Macmillan).

And the Sun	٣٨- وَالشَّمْسُ تَجْرِي
Runs his course	لِمُسْتَقَرٍّ لَّهَا
For a period determined	ذَٰلِكَ تَقْدِيرُ
For him:that is	الْعَزِيزِ الْعَلِيمِ ۝
The decree of(Him)	
The Exalted in Might,	
The All-Knowing.	
36(38)	

path, creating an overall chaos in a part of the cosmos. The revelations says:—

"(The Day) when,
The sun is overthrown,
And when the mountains, fly out their **position**
And when the stars fall loosing their light,
. . . .81(1–4).

١ إِذَا ٱلشَّمْسُ كُوِّرَتْ
٢ وَإِذَا ٱلنُّجُومُ ٱنكَدَرَتْ
٣ وَإِذَا ٱلْجِبَالُ سُيِّرَتْ

The scene expressed in these verses represents a catastrophy of much greater size , involving at least a significant portion of our galaxy.It would be a great turbulance, which once initiated, will effect other nearby solar systems.If we try to explain the mechanism of this happening in the light of the current knowledge of astrophysics, it could be caused by the explosion of some supernova[6].One type of such explosion occurs when a massive star exhausts its nuclear fuel and collapses under its own weight. When its matter, falling in from all directions, meet at its centre, a shock wave bounces back in a tremendous explosion that blows apart the star's outermost layers. Star's atmosphere may explode outward at a speed as high as 100 million miles per hour. The energy released in such explosions could be greater than several billion suns, which can effect the nearby stars.

A second type of supernova, may be initiated by the explosion of the companion star of the sun. In this case a gravitationally powerful white dwarf star that is part of a binary star system draws gas from its nearby companion. When it accumulates too much matter, on reaching a critical mass about 1.4 times as great as our Sun's, it blows up. There is a remote possibility that one supernova may initiate an-other supernova resulting into a chain reaction of heavenly explosions. The verses 81(1-4) seem to refer to this type of chain reaction at the time of the Doomsday of the sun : pictures of the explosions in some remote worlds are shown in the Fig. 24.

PASSIVE AND OF THE SOLAR SYSTEM

Above was a highly dynamic mechanism of the end of our Solar system. However a passive theory[9] of the end of the solar system is based upon the consumption of hydrogen in the atmosphere of the sun, which is its fuel and is consumed in the atomic fusion reactions responsible for the creation of enormous amount of its energy. According to Paul Davies[10], the scenario of this awful

Doomsday is as follows

"As far as our local region of the universe is concerned the fate of the Earth is intimately linked with the fate of the sun. Earth life feeds on sunlight, and any major disruption to the sun's present quiescence will spell disaster. There is no lack of possible solar twitches that could render the earth uninhabitable. Any alteration in the sun's constant heat output could upset the Earth's delicate climatic balance and plunge us into a catastrophic ice age. Changes in the magnetic patterns of the solar system connected with the so-called solar wind — a steady stream of particles from the sun's surface-might bring about equally drastic change. The explosion of a nearby star could drench us in lethal radiation, or the passage of a black hole through the solar system might rock the planets in their orbits".

"But assuming the Earth escapes all these unpleasant possibilities. it is clear that things cannot continue as now 'for ever and ever'. The prolific radiation of energy by the sun has to be paid for in nuclear fuel, and eventually the fuel reserves will start to run out. Astrophysicists estimate that this will not happen for another four to five billion years, which may seem a large length of time. However, by comparison to the age of the universe of eighteen billion years, it is a little period."

"As the fuel runs low, so the sun will swell up, turning into the sort of star that astronomers call a red giant. At a stage the sun will become so big that the inner planets will be engulfed, the Earth's atmosphere stripped away and the solid rocks melted or even vaporized" Fig.15: is a graphical representation of these events.

"Thereafter, the sun will embark on a new and erratic career, in which the nuclear burning of hydrogen fuel, so prolific today, will be replaced by the less efficient burning of helium, and thence by heavier and heavier elements. When finally all fuel is exhausted, the sun will consist of moderately heavy elements such as iron. Any further fusion of nuclei would not result in the release of energy. Iron is the most stable nuclear form, and according to the secord law of thermodynamics, all systems seek out their most stable state. During this phase the sun's central temperature will have risen steadily towards a billion degrees. Now, with all fuel spent, the internal pressure will falter and gravity will take command The aged sun will start to contract under its own weight, crushing

Fig. 28: Relative speed and position of our solar system in the Milky Way.

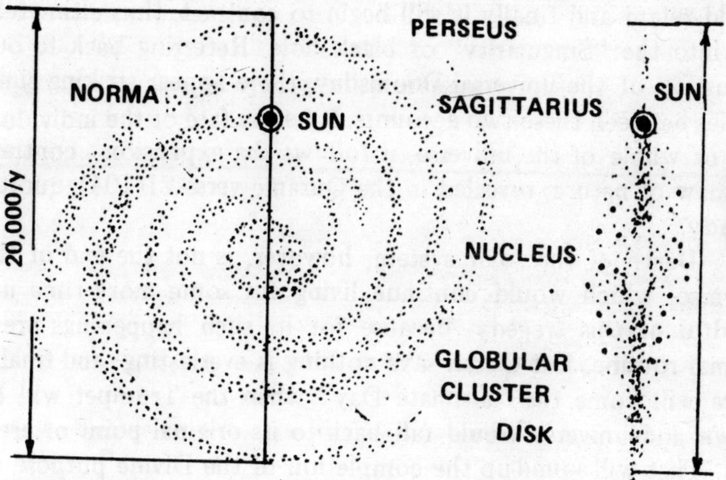

Universe consists of millions of Galaxies. Our Milky Way is one out of those millions. In it are trillions of stars like our sun. Each sun has several plannets. Doomsday of each of these worlds is a separate event. The Fig. shows the main part of the Milky Way Galaxy nucleous halo and dish. The Sun is about 33,000 light year from the centre. The spiral shape shows that once all this mass was concentrated at the centre of the galaxy. Some day it may roll back and destroy itself, following the general principle of creation, evolution and destruction given by the Quranic Verse 21 (104).

"There would be a Day,
When We shall roll up the heavens,
Like a recorder rolls up a written scroll,
As We began the first creation,
We shall repeat it,
It is a promise upon us,
Lo! We are to perform it"
. . . .21(104).

١٠٤ يَوْمَ نَطْوِي السَّمَاءَ كَطَيِّ السِّجِلِّ لِلْكُتُبِ
كَمَا بَدَأْنَا أَوَّلَ خَلْقٍ نُعِيدُهُ
وَعْدًا عَلَيْنَا
إِنَّا كُنَّا فَاعِلِينَ ۝

the material within it so violently that the density will rise to a million grams per cubic centimetre, slowly fading and cooling to end its career as a black dwarf star".

Briefly this scientific scenario means that at present Sun is expanding in volume, which after having reached a maximum, would retard and finally it will begin to contract, thus ultimately end into the "Singularity" of black hole. Referring back to our discussion of the universal Doomsday, there appear striking similarities between these two accounts. It be the fate of the individual star or whole of the universe, it follows the expansion - contraction law of nature; revealed in the Quranic verse 21(104), quoted already.

Death of the solar system, however, is not the end of the universe, which would continue living for some more time unmindful of this tragedy, because, for it, such happenings are a normal routine. But Quran says nothing is everlasting; and finally there will come the "ultimate Day" when the Trumpet will be blown and universe would fall back to its original point of creation. That will sound up the completion of the Divine purpose of the first order of existence; and the beginning of the new order of everlasting existence.

"Are thou not aware of the fact,
That God has created the heavens and the earth
In accordance with a Divine purpose
He can, if He so wills, do away with you,
And bring forth an entirely new creation,
It is not difficult for God"
. . . 14(19–20)

١٩. أَلَمْ تَرَ أَنَّ اللّٰهَ خَلَقَ السَّمٰوٰتِ وَالْأَرْضَ
بِالْحَقِّ ۚ إِنْ يَّشَأْ يُذْهِبْكُمْ
وَيَأْتِ بِخَلْقٍ جَدِيْدٍ ۝
٢٠. وَمَا ذٰلِكَ عَلَى اللّٰهِ بِعَزِيْزٍ ۝

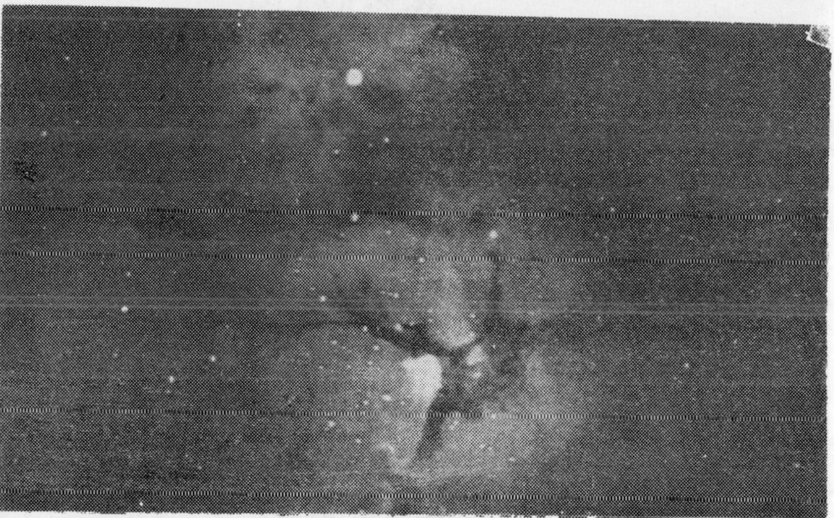

Fig.24: Above is the picture of the two of the great Nebula taken from earth. Now they are simply very hot plasma of gases. But once they could have been the worlds like our solar system. At their turn they had their Doomsday. At our turn we shall see our own Doomsday.. While the old stars die, new stars are created from the gaseous materials left over from the previous generation of stars. This process will continue till the Universal Doomsday which according to some estimates is about 10 billion years away.

٨ وَكَأَيِّن مِّن قَرْيَةٍ عَتَتْ عَنْ أَمْرِ
رَبِّهَا وَرُسُلِهِۦ فَحَاسَبْنَٰهَا حِسَابًا
شَدِيدًا وَعَذَّبْنَٰهَا عَذَابًا نُّكْرًا

٩ فَذَاقَتْ وَبَالَ أَمْرِهَا وَكَانَ
عَٰقِبَةُ أَمْرِهَا خُسْرًا

١٠ أَعَدَّ ٱللَّهُ لَهُمْ عَذَابًا شَدِيدًا فَٱتَّقُوا۟ ٱللَّهَ
يَٰٓأُو۟لِى ٱلْأَلْبَٰبِ ٱلَّذِينَ ءَامَنُوا۟ قَدْ
أَنزَلَ ٱللَّهُ إِلَيْكُمْ ذِكْرًا

"And how many a community revolted
against the ordinance of its Lord,
And His messenger,
And We called it to a stern account,
And punished it with dire punishment,
So that it tasted the ill effects
of its conduct,
And the consequences of its conduct was loss.
Allah has prepared for them stern
punishment(in the hereafter also),
So keep your duty to Allah,
O'ye who believe,
Now Allah has sent down you
a Reminder"

65(8-10)

Chapter-16.

THE SECOND BEGINNING; THE NEW UNIVERSE

It was discussed in the beginning of this book that Doomsday of earth is but just one of the series of such catastrophic events which regularly occur among the innumerable worlds like it, in this extremely vast universe. On the universal scale such events may be termed as minor disturbances in the vastness of the cosmos. In fact, our Doomsday would not be a significant event even in our own Milky Way which is but one out of millions of galaxies in the heavens, and is thought to have well over a billion solar systems like ours. Many of these are supposed to have living worlds also. Each one of them, at their turn must have its accountability also. Ultimately, there would come the time when whole of the universe would be turned off. That will be the beginning of the reversal of time and space, a phase change from the expansion of universe to its constraction. That will mark the beginning of the "Ultimate Doomsday", implosion of which would result into re-explosion of the contracting universe, which in turn will sound the beginning of the New Universe.

"Are thou not aware of the fact,
That God has created the heavens and the earth
In accordance with a Divine purpose.
He can, if He so wills, do away with you,
And bring forth an entirely new creation,
It is not difficult for God"-
. . . .14(19–20(

١٩ الم تر ان الله خلق السموت والارض
بالحق ان يشا يذهبكم ويات بخلق
جديد
٢٠ وما ذلك على الله بعزيز

Process of rebuilding after the ultimate Doomsday was promised in the Holy Quran in its following revelation:—

"As We began the first creation,
Surely We shall repeat it,
It is a promise upon Us,
Lo! We are to perform it"
. . . .21(104)

كما بدانا اول خلق
نعيده وعدا علينا انا كنا فعلين

It is of great scientific interest that recreated universe will not be a replica of the present one, but a grand system of new heavenly bodies, very much different from the present one. In this respect the following revelation is highly thought provoking:—

"Earth will be changed,
To a different earth,
And so will be the heavens"
. . . .14(48)

٤٨ يَوْمَ تُبَدَّلُ الْأَرْضُ غَيْرَ الْأَرْضِ
وَالسَّمٰوٰتُ

We also see in the Holy Quran that the new universe will be divisible into three broad regions. The paradise (جنت), Neutral (اعراف), and the Hell (جہنم). Paradise will be the permanent abode of the universal community of the righteous people of all the times, of all the worlds. In size, says Holy Quran, it is unimaginably big:—

"A Paradise
where of the breadth is,
As the breadth of
The (present) heavens and earth,
which is there,
For those who believe"
. . . .57(21)

٢١ سَابِقُوٓا۟ إِلَىٰ مَغْفِرَةٍ مِّن رَّبِّكُمْ وَجَنَّةٍ
عَرْضُهَا كَعَرْضِ السَّمَآءِ وَالْأَرْضِ أُعِدَّتْ لِلَّذِينَ
ءَامَنُوا۟ بِاللَّهِ وَرُسُلِهِۦ ذَٰلِكَ فَضْلُ اللَّهِ يُؤْتِيهِ
مَن يَشَآءُ وَاللَّهُ ذُو الْفَضْلِ الْعَظِيمِ

In this verse, the comparison of the Paradise with the present heavenly worlds show that its size would be too big to imagine. The one heaven of which science has got some idea, is estimated to consist of millions of galaxies, whereas each galaxy is approximately an island of 100 billion stars. Its width being so big that light travelling at a speed of 1,86,000 miles per second, takes nearly 20,000 years to reach from its one end to the other. From here imagine the size of the heaven and earths and then imagine the size of the Paradise of the new universe, which is said to be bigger than all this.

Similarly, sizes of the Hell and Neutral should also be very big. Thus, the size of the entire order of the new universe is just beyond any imagination.

This brings us to the important question, whether the new universe will also repeat itself after reaching its age? Answer we see through the Holy Quran is "No; the new universe would be for ever". There are number of Quranic verses which promise the ever living status of the residents of the Paradise, (Thus the next order of the existence is not going to repeat itself). The scientific reason for non-repetitive nature of the new universe may be found in its too big size. For example it has been estimated[17] that if its overall density would have been lower than a certain critical value, present universe would also go on expanding for ever. Same reasoning might be applicable to the everliving character of the new universe.

As for the question, that how will the life begin again; how the dead would be brought back to life; how the resurrection would take place; Holy Quran repeatedly says that it will be in the same manner as had the previous order taken place in the first instant . If this order could come from nothing, why not the second beginning? The revelation 31(38) provides the answer to these fundamental questions in the following words:—

"Your creation and your resurrection,
Is but like that of a single cell,
Verily He is the All-Hearing and Seeing"
. . . .31(28).

٢٨ مَّا خَلْقُكُمْ وَلَا بَعْثُكُمْ
إِلَّا كَنَفْسٍ وَاحِدَةٍ إِنَّ اللَّهَ سَمِيعٌ بَصِيرٌ

People on the Day of Resurrection will suppose that they slept for only a while, and woke up. And it will be a controversial issue for them;

"The guilty will vow that they did tarry
but an hour,
But those to whom knowledge and faith
are given, will say;
The Truth is, ye have tarried by Allah's
decree untill the Day of Resurrection,
This is the Day of Resurrection.
But ye used not to believe"
. . . .30(55–56).

٥٥ وَيَوْمَ تَقُومُ السَّاعَةُ يُقْسِمُ الْمُجْرِمُونَ
مَا لَبِثُوا غَيْرَ سَاعَةٍ
كَذَٰلِكَ كَانُوا يُؤْفَكُونَ
٥٦ وَقَالَ الَّذِينَ أُوتُوا الْعِلْمَ وَالْإِيمَانَ لَقَدْ
لَبِثْتُمْ فِي كِتَابِ اللَّهِ إِلَىٰ يَوْمِ الْبَعْثِ فَهَٰذَا يَوْمُ
الْبَعْثِ وَلَٰكِنَّكُمْ كُنتُمْ لَا تَعْلَمُونَ

٣٨ هذا يوم الفصل جمعنكم والأولين

٣٩ فإن كان لكم كيد فكيدون

٤٠ ويل يومئذ للمكذبين

٤١ إن المتقين في ظلل وعيون

٤٢ وفوكه مما يشتهون

٤٣ كلوا واشربوا هنيئا بما كنتم تعملون

٤٤ إنا كذلك نجزي المحسنين

٤٥ ويل يومئذ للمكذبين

٤٦ كلوا وتمتعوا قليلا إنكم مجرمون

٤٧ ويل يومئذ للمكذبين

٤٨ وإذا قيل لهم اركعوا لا يركعون

٤٩ ويل يومئذ للمكذبين

٥٠ فبأي حديث بعده يؤمنون

"This is the Day of Decision,
We have brought you and the men of old together.
If now ye have any wit,outwit Me.
Woe unto the repudiators on that day!
Lo!those who kept their duty are amid shade and fountains
And fruits such as they desire.
(Unto them it is said:)Eat,drink and welcome,
O ye blessed,in return for what ye did.
Thus do We reward the good.
Woe unto the repudiators on that day!
Eat and take your ease(on earth)a little.
Lo!ye are guilty.
Woe unto the repudiators on that day!
When it is said unto them:
Bow down,they bow not down!
Woe unto the repudiators on that day!
In what statement,after this,will they believe?

77(38-50)

Chapter-17

SOME REFLECTIONS OF THE DAY OF RESURRECTION AS TOLD BY THE PROPHET OF ALLAH

45

Narrated Abu Sa id Al-Khudri: We said, "O Allah s Apostle! Shall we see our Lord on the Day of Resurrection? He said, "Do you have any difficulty in seeing the sun and the moon when the sky is clear?" We said, "No" He said, So you will have no difficulty in seeing your Lord on that Day as you have no difficulty in seeing the sun and the moon (in a clear sky)". The Prophet than said, "Somebody will then announce, "Let every nation follow what they used to worship".So the companions of the cross will go with their cross, and the idolators (will go) with their idols, and the companions of every god (false deities) will go) with their god, till there remain those who used to worship Allah, both the obedient ones and the mischievous ones, and some of the people of the Scripture. Then Hell will be presented to them as if it were a mirage. Then it will be said to the Jews, "What did you use to worship?" They will reply, "We used to worship Ezra, the son of Allah. It will be said to them, You are liars, for Allah has neither a wife nor a son. What do you want (now)? They will reply, "We want You to provide us with water". Then it will be said to them 'Drink', and they will fall down in Hell (instead). Then it will be said to the Christians, "What did you use to worship? They will reply, 'We used to worship Messiah, the son of Allah. It will be said, "You are liars, for Allah has neither a wife nor a son. What do you want (now)? They will say, We want You to provide us with water. It will be said to them, 'Drink', and they will fall down in Hell (instead). When there remain only those who used to worship Allah (Alone), both the obedient ones and the mischievous ones, it will be said to them, What keeps you here when all the people have gone? They will say, We parted with them (in the world) when we were in greater need of them than we are today, we heard the call of one proclaiming, 'Let every nation follow what they used to worship, and now we are waiting for our Lord. Then the Almighty will come to them in a shape other than the one which they saw the first time, and He will say, I am your Lord, and they will say, You are our Lord. And none will speak to Him then but the

Prophets, and then it will be said to them, Do you know any sign by which you can recognise Him? They will say, 'The Nur', and so Allah will then uncover His Shine whereupon every believer will prostrate before Him and there will remain those who used to prostrate before Him just for showing off and for gaining good reputation. These people will try to prostrate but their backs will be rigid like one piece of a wood (and they will not be able to prostrate) Then the bridge will be laid across Hell." We, the companions of the Prophet said, 'O Allah s Apostle! What is the bridge? He said, "It is a slippery (bridge) on which there are clamps and (Hooks like) a thorny seed that is wider at one side and narrow at the other and has thorns with bent ends. Such a thorny seed is found in Najd and is called As Sa'dan. Some of the believers will cross the bridge as quickly as the wink of an eye, some others as quick as lightning, a strong wind, fast horses or she-camels. So some will be safe without any harm; some will be safe after receiving some scratches, and some will fall down into Hell (Fire). The last person will cross by being dragged (over the bridge)". The Prophet(S.A.W.) said, "You (Muslims) cannot be more pressing in claiming from me a right that has been clearly proved to be yours than the believers in interceding with Almighty for their (Muslim) brothers on that Day, when they see themselves safe. They will say, "O Allah! (Save) our brothers (for they) used to pray with us, fast with us and also do good deeds with us. Allah will say, "Go and take out (of Hell) anyone in whose heart you find faith equal to the weight of one (gold) Dinar". Allah will forbid the Fire to burn the faces of those sinners. They will go to them and find some of them in Hell (Fire) up to their feet, and some up to the middle of their legs. So they will take out those whom they will recognise and then they will return, and Allah will say (to them), "Go and take out (of Hell) anyone in whose heart you find faith equal to the weight of one half Dinar". They will take out whomever they will recognise and return, and then Allah will say, "Go and take out (of Hell) anyone in whose heart you find faith equal to the weight of an atom (or a smallest ant), and so they will take out all those whom they will recognise". Abu Sa'id said: If you do not believe me then read the Holy Verse:—

"Surely! Allah wrongs not even of the weight of an atom (or a smallest ant) but if, there is any good (done) He doubles it". (4.40)

The Prophet (S.A.W.) added, "Then the prophets and Angels and the believers will intercede, and (last of all) the Almighty (Allah) will say, "Now remains My Intercession. He will then hold a handful of the Fire from which He will take out some people whose bodies have been burnt, and they will be thrown into a river at the entrance of Paradise, called the water of life. They will grow on its banks, as a seed carried by the torrent grows. You have noticed how it grows beside a rock or beside a tree, and how the side facing the sun is usually green while the side facing the shade is white. Those people will come out (of the River of Life) like pearls, and they will have (golden) necklaces, and then they will enter Paradise whereupon the people of Paradise will say, "These are the people emancipated by the Beneficent. He has admitted them into Paradise without them having done any good deeds and without sending forth any good (for themselves). Then it will be said to them, "For you is what you have seen and its equivalent as well", (Bukhari).

Narrated Anas: The Prophet said, " The believers will be kept (waiting) on the Day of Resurrection so long that they will become worried and say, "Let us ask somebody to intercede for us with our Lord so that He may relieve us from our place. Then they will go to Adam and say.,' You are Adam, the father of the people. Allah created you with His Own Hand and made you reside in His Paradise and ordered His angels to prostrate before you, and taught you the names of all things. Will you intercede for us with your Lord so that He may relieve us from this place of ours? Adam will say, I am not fit for this undertaking. He will mention his mistakes he had committed, i.e. his eating off the tree though he had been forbidden to do so. He will add, "Go to Noah, the first prophet sent by Allah to the people of the Earth". The people will go to Noah who will say, "I am not fit for this undertaking". He will mention his mistake which he had done, i.e. his asking his Lord without knowledge. He will say (to them,) "Go to Abraham, Khalil Ar Rahman. They will go to

Abraham who will say, "I am not fit for this undertaking. He would mention three words by which he told a lie, and say (to them). "Go to Moses, a slave whom Allah gave the Torah and spoke to, directly and brought near Him, for conversation". They will go to Moses who will say, "I am not fit for this undertaking. He will mention his mistake he made, i.e. killing a person, and will say (to them), "Go to Jesus, Alla's slave and His Apostle, and a soul (Rouh-ullah) created by Him and His Word". (Be: And it was). They will go to Jesus who will say, I am not fit for this undertaking but you'd better go to Muhammad the slave whose past and future sins have been firgiven by Allah. So they will come to me, and I will ask my Lord's permission to enter His House and then I will be permitted. When I see Him I will fall down in prostration before Him, and He will leave me (in prostration) as long as He will, and then He will say, " O Muhammad, lift up your head and speak, for you will be listened to, and intercede, for your intercession will be accepted, and ask (for anything) for it will be granted. "Then I will raise my head and glorify my Lord with certain praises which He will teach me. Allah will put a limit for me (to intercede for a certain type of people). I will take them out and make them enter Paradise". (Qatada said: I heard Anas saying that), the Prophet said, "I will go and take them out of Hell (Fire) and let them enter Paradise, and then I will return and ask my Lord for permission to enter His House and I will be permited. When I will see Him I will fall down in prostration before Him and He will leave me in prostration as long as He will let me (in that state), and then He will say, 'O Muhammad, raise your head and speak, for you will be listened to, and intercede, for your intercession will be accepted, and ask, your request will be granted. "The Prophet(S.A.W.) added, "So I will raise my head and glorify and praise Him as He has taught me. Then I will intercede and He will put a limit for me (to intercede for a certain type of people). I will take them out and let them enter Paradise". (Qatada added: I heard Anas saying that) the Prophet (S.A.W.) said, "I will go and take them out of Hell (Fire) and let them enter Paradise, and I will retun for the third time and will ask my Lord for permission to enter His house, and I will be allowed to enter. When I see Him, I will fall down in prostration before Him, and will remain in prostration as long as He will, and then He will say, "Raise your head, O Muhammad, and speak, for you will be listened to, and intercede, for your intercession will be accepted, and ask, for your request will be granted". So I will raise my head and praise Allah as He has taught me and then I will intercede and He will put a limit for me (to intercede for a certain type of people). I will take them out and let them enter Paradise".,(Qatada said: I heard Anas saying that) the Prophet (S.A.W.) said, "So I will go and take them out of Hell (Fire) and let them enter Paradise, till none will remain in the Fire except those whom Quran will imprison (i.e. those who are destined for enternal life in the fire)". The narrator then recited the Verse: "It may be that your Lord will raise you to a Station of Praise and Glory".. (17-79).

The narrator added: This is the Station of Praise and Glory which Allah has promised to your Prophet (S.A.W.). (Bukhari)

٥ وَإِن تَعْجَبْ فَعَجَبٌ قَوْلُهُمْ أَءِذَا كُنَّا تُرَابًا
أَءِنَّا لَفِي خَلْقٍ جَدِيدٍ أُولَٰئِكَ الَّذِينَ كَفَرُوا
بِرَبِّهِمْ وَأُولَٰئِكَ الْأَغْلَالُ فِي أَعْنَاقِهِمْ
وَأُولَٰئِكَ أَصْحَابُ النَّارِ هُمْ فِيهَا خَالِدُونَ

"And if thou wonder,
Then wondrous is their saying:
When we are dust,
Are we then to be raised in
a new creation?
Such are they who disbelieve
in their Lord,
Such have carcans on their necks;
Such are rightful owners of the Fire,
They will abide therein"

13(5)

Chapter-18

THE RESURRECTION AND LIFE IN THE NEW UNIVERSE

Life after Resurrection, that is in the next order of existence is a place of refinement, reward and punishment, depending on the state of spiritual development at which the human souls leave at the end of their wordly life. That determines their place and level of entry in the new universe. For the souls in peace with their Creator, there is a place called Jannat, struggle there would be to get closer and closer to their Creator, ever and ever.

Along side the state of Paradise, there is the opposite order of existence called Jahannum (جہنم) i.e. the Hell, a place of refinement, a melting pot for the purification of souls. In it though the process is painful, gradually the souls are purified from the evil which had opaqued for them the light of their Creator. They will remain in the hell according to a Divine decree. but finally they would also move up, from Jahannam to the ultimate goal of paradise. In between these two states there is also a neutral state of existence, a state of preparation to enter the paradise.

Life in the New Universe is thus not going to be without the urge to go up. As we have inclination in this world for the riches and recognition, souls in the next world would yearn for achieving nearness to God. Prophet of Allah said, ultimate state of satisfaction in the paradise will be to enter into Noor of Allah; the very Cause of the heavens and earth and of everything therein. Effort, struggle and urge will thus continue for ever with man, both in the Hell and in the Paradise.

Climax of the Doomsday is the very Day of Resurrection, the Day of Accountability (یوم الحساب), which will be again sounded by the Soor, a signal for the rising of the dead from their graves, which is the after-death dream-like phase of existence of the souls, called Burzakh (23(100). At the time of death, they pass into this phase. In the Burzakh, it is said that, there is no real reward or punishment but only the thoughts of the past deeds and reflections of the pending fate of the future; sufficient to keep one's soul happy or unhappy according to their deeds. This state will end suddently on the final call of accountability, the 2nd Soor ( ), which might be the very sound of the great implosion itself. Holy Quran puts this in the following manner:—

"Surely it will need
but one shout,
And Lo!
They will be awakened,
(out of their graves")
....79(13–14)

﴿١٣﴾ فَإِنَّمَا هِيَ زَجْرَةٌ وَاحِدَةٌ
﴿١٤﴾ فَإِذَا هُم بِالسَّاهِرَةِ

All people, of all the generations, of all the times, from every-where in the universe, will come rushing on this call swarming to the place of their ultimate Judgement. The scene is depicted in the verse 101(4):—

" It is a Day on which,
All mankind would be like
the thickly scattered moths.
....101(4)

﴿٤﴾ يَوْمَ يَكُونُ النَّاسُ
كَالْفَرَاشِ الْمَبْثُوثِ

It would be the state of waiting in the Court of the Judge, Who cannot be cheated, Who knows everything, Who is All-Powerful, the Ultimate Sovereign, the Creator of time and space, but the Most Compassionate One. In anguish, people will be reflecting on their past lives and pass judgements on themselves The very thought of mis-deeds would be horryfying, putting them into shame. In this regard the following revelations offer vivid reflections of the last Hour of the Day of Judgement:—

"On that Day,
Hearts beat painfully,
While eyes down cast"
...79(8–9)

﴿٨﴾ قُلُوبٌ يَوْمَئِذٍ وَاجِفَةٌ
﴿٩﴾ أَبْصَارُهَا خَاشِعَةٌ

"Thy Lord shall come,
with angels, rank upon rank;
And the hell is brought nearer"
. . . .89(22–23)

٢٢ وَجَآءَ رَبُّكَ وَٱلْمَلَكُ صَفًّا صَفًّا

٢٣ وَجِاْىٓءَ يَوْمَئِذٍۭ بِجَهَنَّمَ

"And paradise is brought near"
. . . .81(13)

١٣- وَإِذَا ٱلْجَنَّةُ أُزْلِفَتْ

It is then that;

"Every soul will know,
What it has made ready"
. . . .81(14)

١٤- عَلِمَتْ نَفْسٌ مَّآ أَحْضَرَتْ

"Who so does good, an atom's weight,
Will see it then,
And who so does ill, an atom's weight,
Will see it then"
. . . .99(7–8)

٧ فَمَن يَعْمَلْ مِثْقَالَ ذَرَّةٍ خَيْرًا يَرَهُۥ

٨ وَمَن يَعْمَلْ مِثْقَالَ ذَرَّةٍ شَرًّا يَرَهُۥ

And then:—

"As for him,
Whose scales are heavy (with good works)
He will live in a pleasant state,
But as for, whose scales are light,
The brefet and hungry will be his abode,
Ah, what will convey thee, what she is,
A raging fire"
. . . .101(6–11)

٦ فَأَمَّا مَن ثَقُلَتْ مَوَٰزِينُهُۥ

٧ فَهُوَ فِى عِيشَةٍ رَّاضِيَةٍ

٨ وَأَمَّا مَنْ خَفَّتْ مَوَٰزِينُهُۥ

٩ فَأُمُّهُۥ هَاوِيَةٌ

١٠ وَمَآ أَدْرَىٰكَ مَا هِيَهْ ١١ نَارٌ حَامِيَةٌۢ

It is in view of this pending fate that, Holy Quran advises mankind to prepare for the unending years to come and enter into the next life with the proper development of soul so that it may easily adjust in the new environments. Period of the worldly life is the preparation time for the same. But it is strange that while we put all our efforts for our body comforts, we neglect the soul which does not die. Thus we betray our own selves and work against our own eternal interest. Why so that man cannot see beyond the worldy life of a counted few years? If we have to go even for a day away from our homes, we prepare well for the journey, but when it comes to the journey of eternity, we do not bother at all. Why is that?

The reason may be simple, that we do not know our realselves. But, is that an acceptable excuse, especially in these days when we spend so much of our time, money and effort for our education in the worldly affairs, but hardly we spare few moments to know about the world to come? We profoundly believe in the professors of physical sciences but doubt the beneficient well wishers who spend whole of their life in the search of eternal truths of life. Does it appeal to the common sense?

Strangely enough, though most of the man's worldly knowledge is the acquired knowledge from others, but as it comes to spiritual matters, he refuses to believe in the specialists of these fields and says, if what they say is right; God should have sent His revelation directly on me. This is the same what people had said in the past also. They believe in the law of conservation of matter and energy, but when it comes to themselves they are confused. If matter lives, then atoms of our body are not going to be destroyed also. If energy is eternal our soul cannot be mortal also.

Those who wish to know their inner reality and believe in God, they are fortunate to have Holy Quran which clearly teaches us about the conservation of soul; and tells about the ways of its development for the future life, where-after there would be no end. In it, is spelled the God's message in the purest form to guide us on the way that leads to our Creator. Not only that, we have also in front of us the life of the last of His Messengers in all its details. Those who follow his foot steps, have no fear of going wrong but those who follow their own desires they are like those who try to re-invent the wheel and have all the chances of going wrong.

"Know that;
Life of this world is,
But play and amusement,
Pomp and mutual boasting,
And rivalry for wealth and children.
Here is a smilitude,
Like the vegetation after rain,
Whereof the growth is pleasing to the tillers,

اعلموا أنما الحيوة الدنيا لعب ولهو
وزينة وتفاخر بينكم وتكاثر في الأموال
والأولاد كمثل غيث أعجب الكفار
نباته ثم يهيج فتراه مصفرا ثم يكون حطاما
وفي الآخرة عذاب شديد ومغفرة من
الله ورضوان

Fig.24: Human Journey on Time.

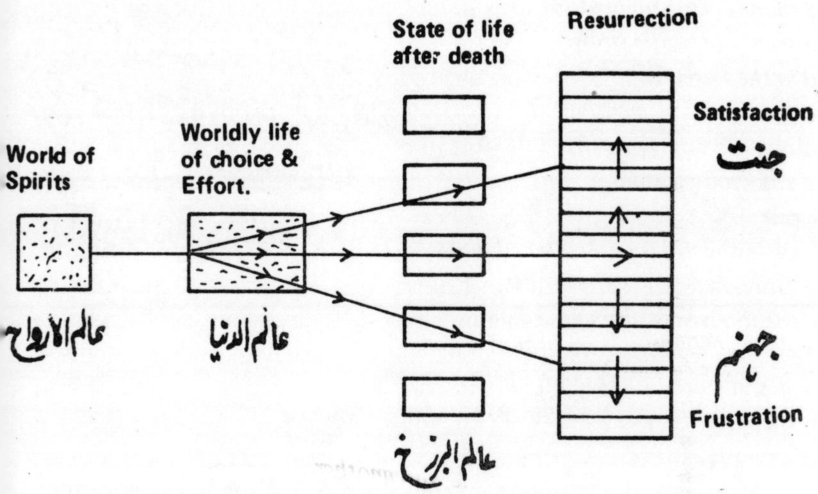

Human soul distinguishes mankind from animals. It is not life, but an "Energy Being", which possibly had its existence in the Pre-universe period also. From that dormant state it takes birth into this world, with the human body as the carrier. This is a period of its free choice and an opportunity for its self development. It departs from the body at the time of death at varying degree of developments as per its choice and effort in this world of cause and effect. In its next existence, in the world of Quabar (برزخ) or Burzakh, it continues with the momentum and direction which it had gathered in its worldly life. Third phase of its existence is after the ultimate Doomsday, the Resurrection. After it will pass into Jannat (جنت) the abode of Happiness and satisfaction; or the Jahanum (جہنم), the abode of misery and frustration. Jahanum is also a place of purification and cleanliness. God, out of His immense Bounty may transfer people from here to Jannat also. Period of life in the world is the most valuable, because it is a respite for us to develop our souls or become like the animals through the greed and lust for the worldly gains

٤ لَقَدْ خَلَقْنَا الْإِنسَانَ فِي أَحْسَنِ تَقْوِيمٍ

٥ ثُمَّ رَدَدْنَاهُ أَسْفَلَ سَافِلِينَ

٦ إِلَّا الَّذِينَ آمَنُوا وَعَمِلُوا الصَّالِحَاتِ فَلَهُمْ أَجْرٌ غَيْرُ مَمْنُونٍ

"We have indeed created man,
in the best status
Then We reduced him to the lowest of the low,
Save those who believe and do good works,
and there is a reward unfailing". . . 95(4 - 6).

Soon it withers,
And thou see it turning yellow,
And then it becomes straw.
And in the Hereafter,
There is a grievous punishment,
And also the forgiveness from Allah,
And His good pleasure,
Whereas;
Life of this world is but matter of illusion,
Therefore, race one with another,
For the forgiveness from your Lord"
and for the Paradise where of the earth,
which is in store for those who believe in Allah
and His messengers". . .57(20–21).

وَمَا الْحَيَوٰةُ الدُّنْيَآ إِلَّا مَتَٰعُ الْغُرُورِ
٢١ سَابِقُوٓا إِلَىٰ مَغْفِرَةٍ مِّن رَّبِّكُمْ وَجَنَّةٍ
عَرْضُهَا كَعَرْضِ السَّمَآءِ وَالْأَرْضِ أُعِدَّتْ لِلَّذِينَ
ءَامَنُوا بِاللَّهِ وَرُسُلِهِۦ ذَٰلِكَ فَضْلُ اللَّهِ يُؤْتِيهِ
مَن يَشَآءُ وَاللَّهُ ذُو الْفَضْلِ الْعَظِيمِ

AHADITH

i. Narrated Ibn Umar (رضي الله عنه) Allah's Apostle may peace be upon him, said, If Allah sends punishment upon a nation then it befalls upon the whole population indiscriminately and then they will be resurrected (and judged) according to their deeds" (Bukhari).

ii. Anas said, the prophet of Allah said, "The first portents of the Hour (Day of Doom) will be a fire that will gather the people from the East to West". (Bukhari).

PART–III

THE LIFE, THE RESURRECTION AND THE ACCOUNTABILITY

The following work is an attempt to understand in rational terms the highly complex-,speculative and sensitive subject of the human soul, the life-after-death, and Resurrection. It is based upon the author's own understanding and interpretations of the Holy Quran and of the sayings of the Holy Prophet. As such there is ample room for difference of opinion and also for the improvements. May Allah guide us on the right path and forgive where we err.

Man says what!
When I am dead, shall I
then he raised up alive,
But does not man call to mind
That we created him before out of nothing
So by thy Lord, without doubt, we shall
gather them together,
and also the evil ones,
Then we shall bring them forth,
on their knees around the Hell,
. . . . .19(66–68)

٦٦ وَيَقُولُ الْإِنسَانُ أَءِذَا مَا مِتُّ لَسَوْفَ
أُخْرَجُ حَيًّا
٦٧ أَوَلَا يَذْكُرُ الْإِنسَانُ أَنَّا خَلَقْنَاهُ مِن
قَبْلُ وَلَمْ يَكُ شَيْئًا
٦٨ فَوَرَبِّكَ لَنَحْشُرَنَّهُمْ وَالشَّيَاطِينَ ثُمَّ
لَنُحْضِرَنَّهُمْ حَوْلَ جَهَنَّمَ جِثِيًّا

ETERNAL LIFE

By the Poet Jalal-ud-Din Roomi

(Translated by Sir Muhammad Iqbal)[30]

First man appeared in the class of inorganic things,

Next he passed therefrom into that of plants,

For years he lived as one of the plants,

Remembering nought of his inorganic state so different,

And when he passed from the vegetative to the animal state,

He had no rememberance of his state as a plant,

Except the inclination he felt to the world of plants,

Especially at the time of spring and sweet flowers,

Like the inclination of infants toward their mothers,

Which know not the cause of their inclination to the breast,

Again the great Creator as you know,

Drew man out of the animal into the human state,

Thus man passed from one order of nature to another*

Till he became wise and knowing and strong as he is now,

Of his first souls he has now no rememberance,
And he will be again changed from his present soul

(*) *"And by the Moon,*
When it alters her fall,
That man, from state to state,
Shall ye be surely carried onward"
.... 84(18-19)

وَالْقَمَرِ إِذَا اتَّسَقَ ﴿١٨﴾
لَتَرْكَبُنَّ طَبَقًا عَن طَبَقٍ ﴿١٩﴾

Chapter-19

SECRET OF LIFE

What is the secret of life? This has been a question asked by Mankind since the dawn of civilization. But to no avail. Life is always associcated with intelligence. What is the source of intelligence? These are the fundamental questions concerning the destiny of the human beings also. Poets, philosphers, and scientists, all have said something about them. But the question remain unanswered?

Previously, it was thought that life came to our earth from the outer space. While this view still persists, side by side a popular opinion is that life began here on earth also. In the beginning, it was very hot, unable to support any life. Later, when it cooled and got the atmosphere which in the beginning had consisted mainly of methane, amonia, hydrogen and water vapours, in the presence of ultra violet radiations, cosmic radiations and lightening storms, which are thought to be too severe then, amino acids were generated in the atmosphere of the earth. In 1957, the American scientists John Miller simulated these conditions in laboratory and was successful in showing the traces of amino acids produced in this process thus confirming the hypothesis of life being earth based. Since amino acids are the essential component of the proteins in the cells of living beings, it was concluded that life had thus evolved on earth from its own resources. It is no doubt an important discovery. At least, to some extent we have a plausible explanation of the source of life but the basic question still remains, that how some lifeless elements combine together to produce life? There is no answer to this.

Let us try to find the answer to this mind boggling question in the Holy Quran, because it is the wisdom from the Creator of the worlds. In this paper we shall see that Holy Quran leads us to the very fundamental concepts of nature, from where we may derive the answer to our basic question in very clear terms. Let us therefore look into the following Divine revelations deeply:

"Our Lord is He,
Who gave to each thing,
Its Form and the Nature,
And gave it Guidance"
. . . .20(50)

۝ قَالَ رَبُّنَا الَّذِيٓ أَعْطٰى كُلَّ شَيْءٍ
خَلْقَهٗ ثُمَّ هَدٰى

"Every matter,
has its appointed time
and course"
....54(3)

وَكُلُّ أَمْرٍ مُّسْتَقِرٌّ

These verses have highlighted the following realities of nature;

(a) That every matter has its appointed time and a fixed course for it;

(b) That in every thing God has built its basic characteristics which guide it to its functions;

(c) Obedience to the Divine laws by each and every bit of the universe is in the very nature of things as if they have been pre-programmed to perform their functions according to certain laid down rules and regulations.

This is confirmed by the scientific observations also that the characteristic of obedience to the laws of nature is ingrained in the very nature of matter.

This brings us to the basic question: What forces the apparently lifeless matter to obey the rules of nature? For example, why does Hydrogen and Oxygen under the given conditions, react together always to produce water? Same can be asked for every other chemical reaction. Can we then say that matter at its very fundamentals, knows what to do under a given circumstance? Going further, can we say that an atom is an-intelligent being?

We see from the Holy Quran that answer to this fundamental question should be affirmative. This takes us to another far reaching assumption that, "atom " is not only the fundamental unit of matter, it is also the fundamental living unit of life, having a mind of its own; the basic unit of intelligence.

From the current scientific knowledge we know that atom is the smallest stable fundamental unit of matter. All things are constituted of atoms of various elements. But atoms is also not the fundamental particle. It is further composed of many smaller particles, the complete picture of which is still not fully known. In fact, in the words of the Noble laureate Prof. Abdus Salam, "the deeper we go into it, the more baffled we are"[46]. For example it has been discovered that in their transition from one orbit to another, an electron seems to have some freedom of choice. During this change over, according to the latest quantum theory, an electron skips over the intervening space without passing through it. It is, as if it disappears in one orbit and simultaneously reappears in another. Behaviour of other fundamental particles in the atom also shows some degree of unpredictability. Heisenburg, Principle of uncertainity is an acknowledgement of this reality. One may ask, why this unpredictability; Has the matter some degree of free choice also?

These questions can be answered by the hypothesis of the mind of the matter as pointed out already in our discussion of the verses 20(50), and 54(3), quoted above according to which each thing and there is no exception to this rule, small or big, has a nature, form; and a built-in-guidance. The idea is further elaborated in the verse 17(44) which say that each thing in the universe praises Allah and declares His Glory.

"The seven heavens and the earth (too)
And all beings therein,
Declare His Glory,
There is not a thing,
but celebrates His praises;
And yet
Ye do not understand,
How they declare His glory!
Verily He is often
For-Bearing, Most forgiving"
....17(44).

٤٤ تُسَبِّحُ لَهُ السَّمَٰوَٰتُ السَّبْعُ وَالْأَرْضُ وَمَن
فِيهِنَّ وَإِن مِّن شَيْءٍ إِلَّا يُسَبِّحُ بِحَمْدِهِ
وَلَٰكِن لَّا تَفْقَهُونَ تَسْبِيحَهُمْ
إِنَّهُ كَانَ حَلِيمًا غَفُورًا

Stress on the phrase, "There is not a thing but celebrates His praises, and yet ye do not understand"(ولكن لا تفقهون) is note worthy. It is obvious from here that all things without exception are conscious of God's glory and existence, irrespective of their being living or non-living. Now consciousness is associated with mind or soul of a thing. Therefore, we may say that mechanism by which each thing of the universe declares His glory and celebrates His praises, is actually their fundamental character.

Fig.28. All things have life, but somethings are more living than others.

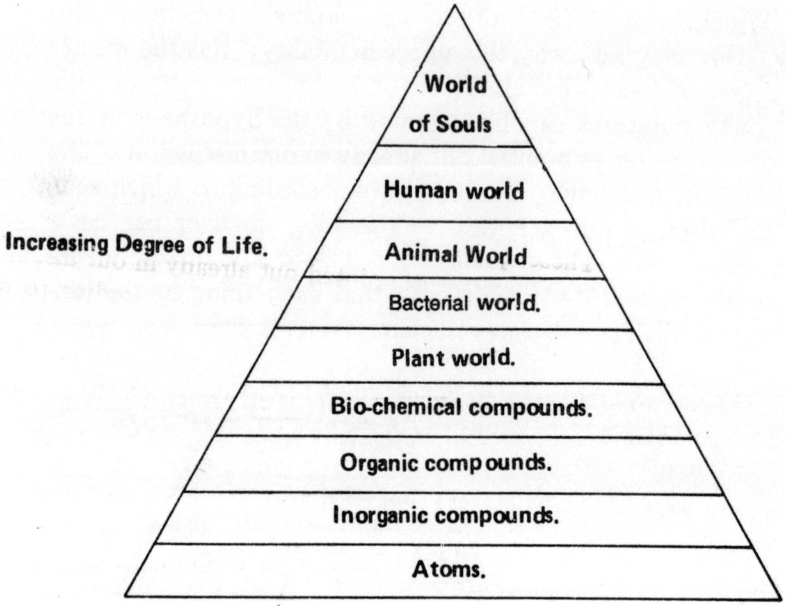

In the absolute terms each things in the nature is living. The lowest living unit of life is the atom itself. It has intelligence and mind of its own, which determines its characteristics and interactions with other atoms of matter. Suitable combinations of atoms, can give birth to higher degrees of life. Thus the state of living and the state of so called non livings things is only relative to each other. Thus life can be created in the labroatory. Human beings manifest the highest degree of life. But still it is due to the bio-chemical combinations of the atoms of their body. However human beings have some thing other the life also, that is their soul whose existence is not dependent upon the body atoms. It is their self which lives for ever.

Since atom is the basic unit of matter, therefore we may say that this characteristic is basic with the atom; i.e. "It is the basic unit of life and has a built-in mind of its own".

This is a revolutionary concept which opens up a new understanding of the nature and provides us the answer to the secret of life. It tells us that why everything hymn the praises of Allah and follow His laws since it needs recognition of a fact, so each thing must have its mind which gives it a character of its own. Through its mind each thing is connected with the Absolute Soul of the Cosmos. Universe is thus an organic unit whose each component, the smallest and biggest, has a built-in mind and a guidance system, which governs its characteristics, behaviour, nature and form. In this scenario atom is the fundamental stable unit of the cosmos. With this hypothesis we can also explain the basis of the life, as no combination of dead atoms could have created life. In this concept each atom of the matter is the fundamental unit of life; and different manifestations of life at various levels of development are thus the outcome of different combinations of atoms. Accordingly the complex molecules would be at a high state of manifestation of life than the simpler ones. Thus we can say that organic compounds are more living than the inorganic one, and within the organic compounds also molecules of more complex compounds represent a higher state of existence. Amino acids which are constituted of even more complex combination of atoms, represent still higher degree of life. And so are their combinations. A living cell is a marvel of the complexity and sophistication of design of the atoms and therefore it is more dynamic than the amino acids. Then the cell of an animal is more complex than the cell of the plant; and the cell of man is much more developed than the cell of an animal i.e. it is at a higher state of life. But in every case the resultant life is the outcome of the life of the atoms which they are composed of. Fig. 25 shows this pyramid of life.

The hypothesis of "Soul and Mind of Matter", leads one to the idea of the trinity of "Time-Space and Mind" as also the regulating system of universe. We know already that nothing is possible without the input of time and space. Thus "Time and Space" allow the happening of events; mind of the matter directs them to their logical conclusions.

Let us illustrate this idea again with the example of formation of water. In this example given the input of time and space, hydrogen and oxygen can react together, but it is the mind of these atoms which under the given conditions decide about the formation of water. Same logic is true for any other compound of matter Interations of Time-Space and Mind is going on since the very beginning. These three are the characteristics of God, manifestations of which is the universe. In the first place they gave birth to energy. Thereafter they regulated it and transformed it into matter. Through this interaction each thing is connected with the Provident.

From elementary matter was evolved the more complex matter which was more dynamic than their constituents, Finally it became what we call living-Mind is free will and the higher animals have more free will than the lower species. Man which is the supreme of creation has the highest degree of free will. We may say that Mind guides the things to their natural behaviour; Time and Space provide them with the basis of their existence. Their working is shown in the Figure-26.

The hypothesis that atom is the basic unit of life with a mind and memory, also means that;

(i) if science can know the chemical arrangement of atoms in a living cell and can rearrange the atoms in the same fashion in the laboratory, then it should be able to reproduce the same living cell. Thus creation of artificial life in the laboratory is an open possibility in the hands of the vicegerents of God on earth.

(ii) Death is the disintegration of the bio-chemical order in the man, but as per the law of conservation of matter atoms of the body never die. Even after disintegration of body, they remain consciousness of their previous life. Therefore with its mind and memory each atom carries the print of its previous life and is a potential candidate for the repetition of its previous life. As such life after death is also an open possibility. Given the suitable envi-ionment, what to say of the Day of Resurrection, it should be possible to reproduce the living from dead from the atoms of their remains.

﴿٢٢﴾ هُوَ اللَّهُ الَّذِي لَا إِلَٰهَ إِلَّا هُوَ عَالِمُ الْغَيْبِ
وَالشَّهَادَةِ هُوَ الرَّحْمَٰنُ الرَّحِيمُ

"He is God, besides whom there is
none who is worthy of being worshipped,
He is the knower of all that is hidden,
and all that is apparent,
He is the most beneficient and Mercifal"
. . . .AlHashar (23).

Above discussion has given birth to a new question and that is, where does the consciousness or mind of the atom resides? Is it in the electron cloud around the nucleous or burried deep into the nucleous? This is question which can be properly answered through scientific analysis and research only. Holy Quran is a beacon light to show us the right direction. The path has to be traced by the seeker himself. And God knows the best.

Hadith and Genetic memory

Narrated Abdullah bin Mas -ud: Allah's Apostle (S.A.W.) the true and truly inspired, narrated to us, 'The creation of everyone of your starts with the process of collecting the material for his body within forty days and forty nights in the womb of his mother. Then he becomes a clot of thick, blood for a similar period (40 days) and then he becomes like a piece of flesh for a similar period. Then an angel is sent to him (by Allah) and the angel is allowed (ordered) to write four things; his livelihood, his (date of) death, his deeds, and whether he will be a wretched one or a blessed one (in the Hereafter) and then the soul is breathed into him. So one of you may do (good) deeds characteristic of the people of Paradize so much that there is nothing except a cubit between him and Paradise but then what has been written for him decides his behaviour and he starts doing (evil) deeds characteristic of the people of Hell (Fire) and (ultimately) enters Hell (Fire); and one of you may do (evil deeds characteristic of the people of Hell (Fire) so much so that there is nothing except a cubit between him and Hell (Fire), then what has been written for him decides his behaviour and he starts doing (good) deeds characteristic of the people of Paradise and (ultimately)enters paradise'.

Does not this Hadith of the Prophet of Allah, point towards the GENETIC CODE, pre-programmed in the living cell of every one?

Fig.26 Working of the Singularity of Time, Space and Mind.

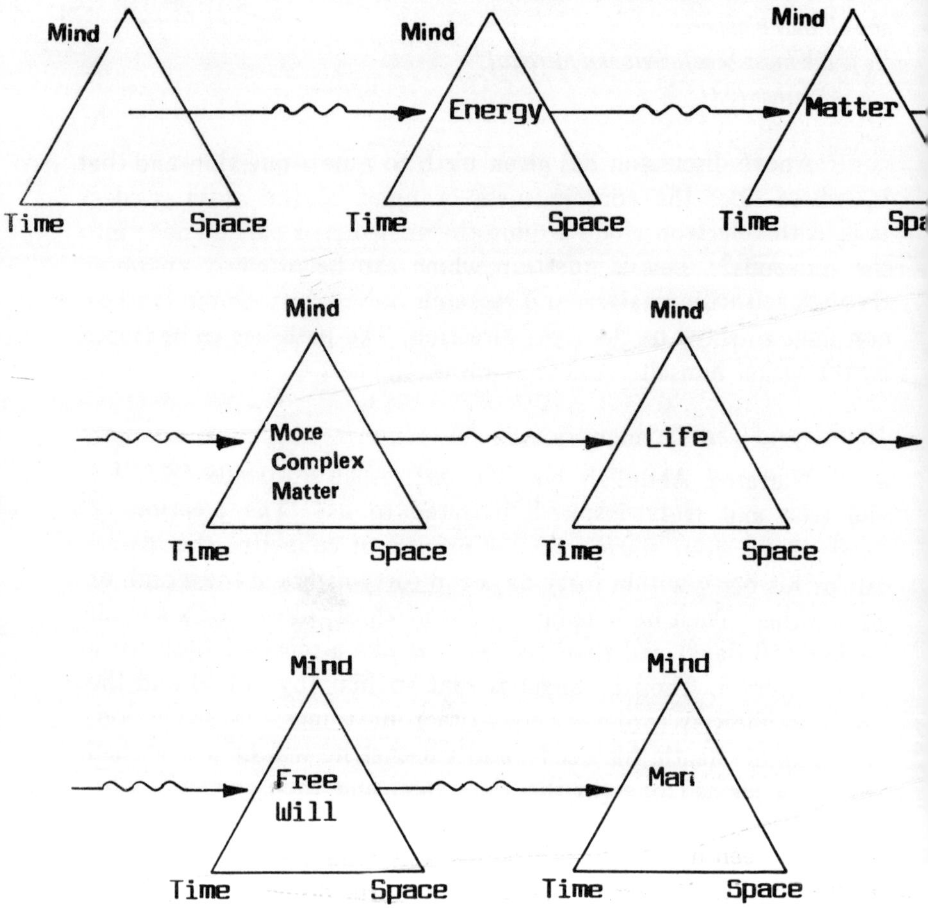

Mind guides the things to their natural behaviour; Time and Space provide them with the basis of their existence. Events thus first of all take place in the Mind of things and therefrom they are transformed into physical shapes. A superior mind can guide an inferior mind. Human beings which have the most developed mind has the potential to guide all other things. Thus predominance of mind, matter, space and time over matter explains; how the moral causes precedes the physical causes; how the physical misfortunes and catastrophies falling on individuals, societies and nations, are triggered by their moral degrations and wicked deeds, as discussed in the Chapter 3 of this Book.

Chapter-20

LIFE AFTER DEATH

Concepts of Life After Death

Question of life after death is one of the most intriguing riddle about the human beings which has been believed by them always but never understood. Even the most primitive societies, like the Abriginoes of Australia believe in the ancestral spirits and beseach them for help while in distress. Among the advanced religions such as Judaism, christianity and Islam this is the fundamental concept of their philosophies. Hindu religions also believe in the reincornation of soul according to its performance in the previous life. In short, there is no society on earth which in one way or the other, is without its concept of life after death.

However it is such an intriguing concept which can never be verified in terms of physical measures, though occasionally we do read in the press about the astonishing stories concerning the spirits. We also often hear about the cases who had died and later, after few hours or so came to life again. In this respect, studies of Dr. Robert Moody,[25] reported in his book "Life after Death" are highly thought provoking. In this book he has investigated the cases of about 150 persons who were clinically declared dead but later, miraculously came back to life. The book is the account of interviews of such persons and provides evidence of the continuity of human soul after death.

Apart from the Moody's work, there is a great deal of religious and mystic literature[26,33] available which carry detailed accounts of the matters of life-after-death but this is not a place to go into such details. However, the recent scientific interest in the Extra Sensory perceptions (E.S.P.) have aroused worldwide concern in meta physics which in the language of religion means, matters related to the human spirit and life-after-death.

As for the Holy Quran, its total concept of religion, society, individual and social justice is based upon the concept of life-after-death, which according to it is a continuation of the life of the world, minus the human body. In this concept Doomsday is the legal requirement of the accountability and justice of the deeds which people perform during their worldly existence. During this life one may go un-noticed, un-punished even if he may userp the rights of others, may be injust, may not fulfil his obligations and duties; but in the life-after-death, each one will be paid for his deeds. Thus justice, needs the Doomsday and the life-after-death.

Inspite of this, belief in the Hereafter remains basically a belief in the unknown. However this is not to be equated with ignorance because, after all, most of our convictions, even about the physical world, are not based upon our direct experiences, but are here-say. In the case of life-after-death, disbelievers are faced with the dillima of comprehension. They ask, how could a man revive after death, when his remains have been totally disintegrated and annihilated with time? This question was also repeatedly asked by the opponents of the Holy Prophet Muhammad, may peace and blessing of Allah be upon him. His reply used to be that One who created the first time, has the power to repeat it also. If somebody can create something out of nothing the first time, it should be even easier for him to do it the second time.Holy Quran, in its innumerable revelations has pleaded people to understand the phenomenon of life-after-death in terms of their daily life experiences, such as the cyclic occurance of day and night, the sudden appearance of plant life in the barren desert lands after rain fall; the man's own creation from a drop of fluid and then his rising to youth and decline in the latter years. Then it argues that for Allah Who has created all the heavens and earths, creation of which is a far bigger matter than the creation of an individual, recreation of the man should not be a difficult matter. Holy Quran is full of such scientific arguments to satisfy the wavering minds about their second existence.

On many occasions it has stressed that every thing about the man is being recorded and documented permanently. These records will speak themselves about what he has been doing in his worldly life. With the knowledge of the present day electronics, it is now easy to comprehend that such a thing should not be impossible. If a man can preserve millions of information bits on a tiny crystal of silica, why cannot the Creator of Universe preserve the record of the man to be unfolded in the Hereafter? If a competent engineer can construct a machine from the available design specifications, why cannot the Creator do the same from the records He keeps?

If one believes God, he cannot deny the life-after-death and the Hereafter also. However it would help to believe if we may resolve the issue in terms of the current scientific terms. But this means knowing the secret of life. If one understand this life, he could then comprehend the life-after-death also. Fig. 24. shows the footsteps of human journey in the frame of time and space.

"Is it ye who create them?
or are We the Creator?
It is We have decreed that death should
be your common lot,
Ye! We are not hindered from replacing
you with others, your likes,
Or from creating you again in forms
which ye know not"
.....56(59–61)

٥٩ ءَأَنتُمْ تَخْلُقُونَهُۥٓ أَمْ نَحْنُ ٱلْخَٰلِقُونَ
٦٠ نَحْنُ قَدَّرْنَا بَيْنَكُمُ ٱلْمَوْتَ وَمَا نَحْنُ
بِمَسْبُوقِينَ
٦١ عَلَىٰٓ أَن نُّبَدِّلَ أَمْثَٰلَكُمْ وَنُنشِئَكُمْ فِى
مَا لَا تَعْلَمُونَ

"And when the Trumpet is blown
There will be no more relationship
between them that day,
Nor will one ask after another
Then those whose balance
(of good deeds) is heavy,
They will attain salvation,
But those whose balance is light,
will be those who lost their souls in Hell,
will they not abide?"
.....23(101–103).

١٠١ فَإِذَا نُفِخَ فِى ٱلصُّورِ
فَلَآ أَنسَابَ بَيْنَهُمْ يَوْمَئِذٍ وَلَا يَتَسَآءَلُونَ
١٠٢ فَمَن ثَقُلَتْ مَوَٰزِينُهُۥ
فَأُو۟لَٰٓئِكَ هُمُ ٱلْمُفْلِحُونَ
١٠٣ وَمَنْ خَفَّتْ مَوَٰزِينُهُۥ فَأُو۟لَٰٓئِكَ ٱلَّذِينَ
خَسِرُوٓا۟ أَنفُسَهُمْ فِى جَهَنَّمَ خَٰلِدُونَ

According to the Islamic concept, as discussed in the chapter 18 also, man is a combination of matter, life and Soul. In this combination life is the manifestation of a certain combination of atoms, each one of which is itself a living reality. Death is the disintegration of the combination of natural elements and consequently the end of life also. But soul is an eternal reality, and Order of God, an Energy Being, created even before the figuring of life on earth. Souls are breathed in the body of the empryo at the beginning of life in the womb. With life it flourishes in the directions of the inclination of the mind of the individual. At the death the Energy Being of the Soul leaves the body and directed to its destinations. In the period between the Hereafter and in the Hereafter. The following chapter 21 discusses this subject in its larger perspectives.

Fig.25:Different States in the Existence of Human Soul.

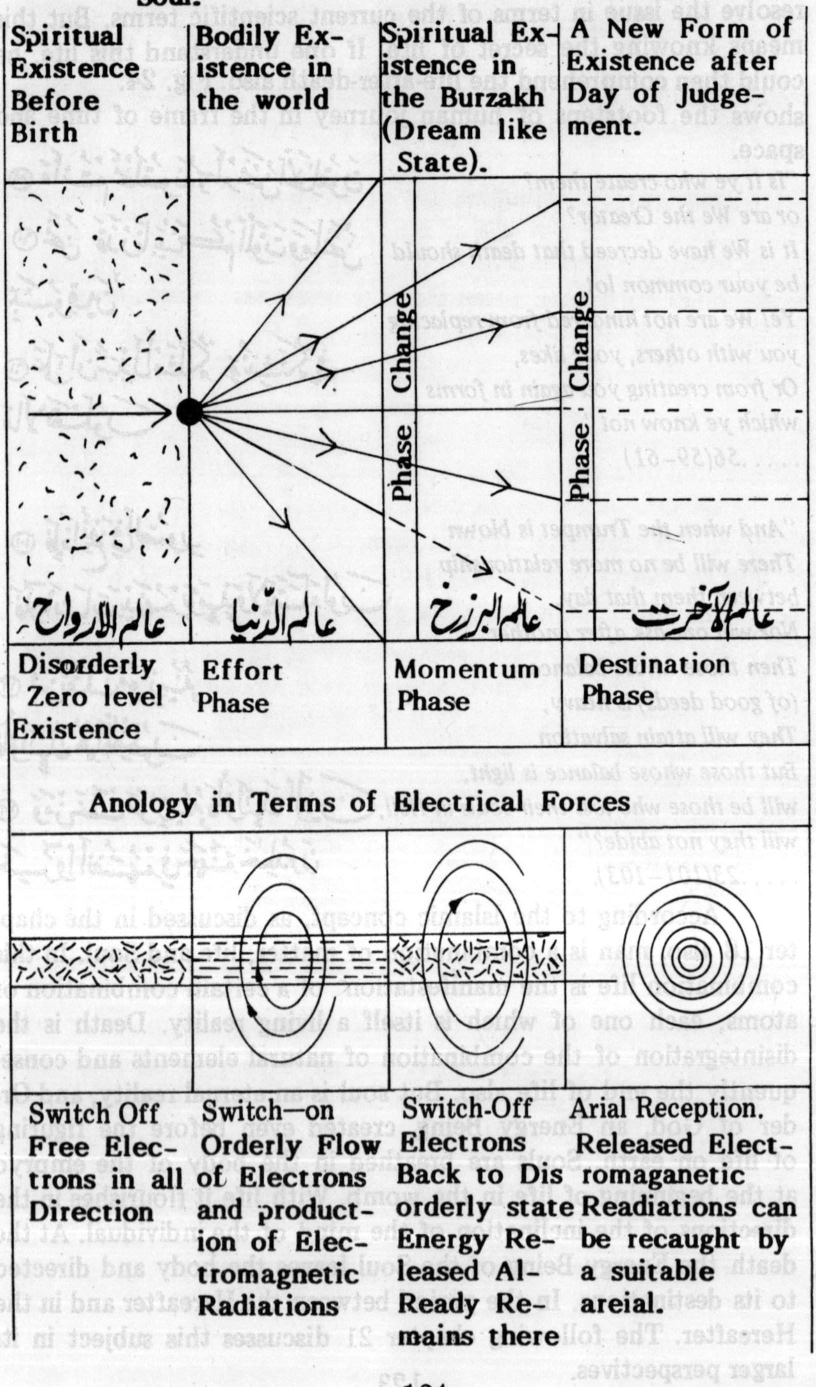

Chapter.21

HUMAN SOUL AND ACCOUNTABILITY

"We have not created,
the heavens and the earth,
And all that is in between them,
For nothing,
Only those who deny (the truth)
imagine so"
. . . .38(27)

٢٧ وَمَا خَلَقْنَا السَّمَاءَ وَالْأَرْضَ وَمَا
بَيْنَهُمَا بَاطِلًا ذَٰلِكَ ظَنُّ الَّذِينَ كَفَرُوا

There are several revelations like the above which lay down purpose as the principle of Creation and the End of the universe. There is a Divine purpose behind everything. Nothing is created for nothing. On this principle Doomsday in the Holy Quran is actually the fulfilment of the purpose of the creation of the whole universe. This is the reason that Quran does not call it "The End", but names it as an "Event" (الساعت) which will change one state of existence into another. As has been said the whole process must follow the calculated scheme of "Divine Will" (امرِ ربی) and in no case is a haphazard accident of nature. Therefore it can be called only as a revolution in the long chain of evolution of the universe which will bring it to a purposeful end; to create a new world as a direct consequence of the present one. This purpose of the Doomsday is revealed by the following revelation:

"Verily the Hour (of the Doom)
is to come;
My design is to keep it hidden,
For every soul to receive its reward,
By the measure of its endeavour"
. . . .20(15)

١٥ إِنَّ السَّاعَةَ آتِيَةٌ أَكَادُ
أُخْفِيهَا لِتُجْزَىٰ كُلُّ نَفْسٍ بِمَا تَسْعَىٰ

Thus Resurrection would be a day of accomplishment, an event of reward and punishment for all those who would have been ever there in the universe, belonging to this world of ours or to any other world. In this regard Holy Quran guides us on the continuation of the human soul, death being only a transformation for it.

Human Soul and Human Life.

Imam Ghazali,[12] the famous Muslim scholar of the 10th century A.D. made a difference between the human soul and the human life; the latter being the result of bio-chemical reactions of elements, and therefore perishable with their disorder. However soul is a kind of energy being, other than life, which determines the human personality. It is the very "Me", separate to the material elements of the body, something inspired in the fetus externally at a certain stage of its development in the womb of the mother. It is not a static being but a dynamic living being which develops over the passage of time on lines it may choose for itself. A graphical representation of different evolutionary stages of the human soul is shown in Fig.25 and 27.

It takes its birth in the fetus from the dormant state of the pre-birth-existence; Thereafter it enters into the active phase of development in the earthly world. Human body is a vehicle of development for it. Here it rises or falls, from the zero level entry stage to its level of competence and effort, it may put in. After bodily death it looses the ability for further development and continues its journey on the path it had founded for it in the world, without ability to modify its course of action. Prophet of Allah illustrated this by saying that reward in the Hereafter depends on your spiritual state at the time of death. All is well that ends well.

As for the question of the real nature of soul, our knowledge would always remain incomplete. Quran says;

"They ask thee of the soul.
Say, it is an order of your Lord,
You have been given but
little knowledge of this"

۝٨٥ وَيَسْـَٔلُونَكَ عَنِ ٱلرُّوحِ قُلِ ٱلرُّوحُ مِنْ أَمْرِ رَبِّى
وَمَآ أُوتِيتُم مِّنَ ٱلْعِلْمِ إِلَّا قَلِيلًا

... *17(85)*

Thus it should be an impossible task for a human mind to understand itself fully. However the situation should not be totally disappointing also. In the Holy Quran God says: "We have indeed created all things by measures" 54(49). This means that Will of God follows a logical system. He further tells in the Holy Quran, " with Him is the Book of Books " 13 (39). and Laws of nature represent His unchanging written Will.

Therefore, human soul must also be as a consequence of some logical reasons. It is also obvious from the Holy Quran that souls are different from matter. They relate to the category of beings like the Angels and Jinns, which are meta-physical realities, having definite personalities, bestowed with c o n s c i e n c e, mind and individuality. From the Holy Quran we also find that they were there even before God had decided of the creation of man on earth; possibly before the beginning of the material universe. We also interpret that basis of their creation is energy, that is they are a kind of energy-being, without material bodies. As such they have not the limitations which are associated with the material beings, that is the limitations of mass and inertia. One of the class of energy beings are the Jinns, about which Quran says that they were created out of a kind of heat energy, plasma of hot gases; as can be seen from the verses 15(26-27)

"Man, We created from fermanted clav,
Dried tingling hard,
And before that We had created Jinns,
From intense radiated fire"
....15(26-27)

وَلَقَدْ خَلَقْنَا الْإِنسَٰنَ مِن صَلْصَٰلٍ مِّنْ حَمَإٍ مَّسْنُونٍ ﴿٢٦﴾
وَالْجَآنَّ خَلَقْنَٰهُ مِن قَبْلُ مِن نَّارِ السَّمُومِ ﴿٢٧﴾

Angels are also made from another type of energy, much more finer and subtle than the fire; called by the name of "Noor" in the Holy Quran. Prophet of Allah told that souls are also made of "Noor" who before their birth in this world live in some other plane of existence. He said:

> "In their previous existence souls live together as a community. Those which were spiritually close to each other, they remain close to each other here also, Those who were at distant from each other there, they have little affinity to each other here also" .... (BUKHARI)

When we survey the modern literature on the subject of soul, life or mind, we also now find a growing appreciation among scientists that neither mind, nor life, need be limited to organic matter. In a recent extremely speculative but thought provoking Book, "Life Beyond Earth"[10]— the possibilities of extraterrestrial life is reviewed by the physicist Gerald Feinberg and the biochemist Robert Shapiro. They argue the case for life based on plasma, electromagnetic field energy, magnetic fields in neutran stars and variety of other bizarre systems. According to Paul Davies,[10] now consciousness and intelligence are software concepts; it is only the pattern — the organization — that counts, not the medium for its expression. This is very much like Imam Ghazali,[11] who in 10th century argued that body is just a vehicle for the soul, as a horse is for the rider; it is the soul that determines our journey in this life, as the rider guides the travel of the horse in the land. Accountability, therefore, is of the rider, not of the horse. Man is responsible for his action through his souls and not the body which is perishable. Prophet Muhammad (S.A.W.) may peace and blessing, of Allah be upon him, had said "Actions will be judged according to the intentions". The reason being that intentions are made in the souls of the men, and actions are simply their manifestations. Consequently at the time of the death, it is soul, which carries the cumulative effect of the deeds performed during the life period in this world.

"That no one who carries a burden,,	٣٨ أَلَّا تَزِرُ وَازِرَةٌ وِزْرَ أُخْرَىٰ
"bears another's load"	
That a man receives but only	٣٩ وَأَن لَّيْسَ لِلْإِنسَانِ إِلَّا مَا سَعَىٰ
"that for which he strives for,"	٤٠ وَأَنَّ سَعْيَهُ سَوْفَ يُرَىٰ
That his endeavours will be judged	
And only then	٤١ ثُمَّ يُجْزَاهُ الْجَزَاءَ الْأَوْفَىٰ
Will he receive his recompense in full	
And that to your Lord is your returning"	٤٢ وَأَنَّ إِلَىٰ رَبِّكَ الْمُنتَهَىٰ
. . . . 53(38–42).	

There are many people in the world who still do not believe in the continuity of soul or life after death. Their argument is that they cannot comprehend anything like that. However we must acknowledge that soul is not the only secret of nature which we do not comprehend. Their is a whole lot of unseen world around us about which we have little knowledge. The wise acknowledge it as a reality while the fools contest it. They fail to appreciate what the great Newton had said, "His knowledge of the universe is as a drop in the Ocean". And before him Aristotle had said, "I know only that I know not".

Fig. 26: Mankind alone have the souls, Animals only the life.

All living beings are the set of life and matter

All human beings are the set of life, matter and soul.

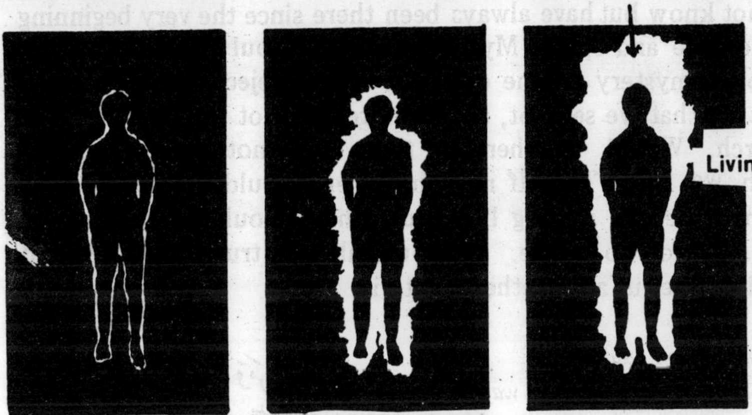

Stunted soul **Relatively Developed Soul** **More Developed Soul**

Soul and life are two different things. Life is due to the bio-chemical combinations of the atoms. which are units of life. For details see Chapter-18. All living beings have life, degree of which is manifested by their knowledge of environment, dynamism and free will. Soul is unique for the human beings only, which give them a character and personality; the choice of good and bad; conscienee and inspiration. Whereas life finishes with the death, the soul never dies. As one can develop his body and life by proper exercise and food; one can also grow his soul or stunt it, but it needs different type of treatment. God sent His prophets. By following their teachings we can also develop our souls. Muhammad, Peace be upon Him, was the last of His Messengers and in this respect, a model for the entire humanity, and the Holy Quran being the lattest edition replaces all the revealed books to the earlier prophets. By following its teachings one can prepare him best for the life to come.

As far the continuity of existence, it is not at all a strange thing. Even in this life we come across hundreds of things which are continuing since time immemorial. Hardly we ever think that hydrogen in the water we drink is actually as old as the universe itself. Carbon in our bodies has come from the explosion of some remote stars of which we have no idea. In every square centimeter of space, solid or vacuum alike, at least 150 particles of neutrinos pass through it every second without our knowledge. Solar energy which gives us life, has its origin in the fusion of hydrogen, which was created in the first second of the life of the universe, some 20 billion years ago.

In fact, there is an unending list of things, which we may not know but have always been there since the very beginning of the time and space. Mystery of human soul is therefore not the only mystery of the creation. If we reject it we ought to reject all that we see not, and comprehend not with our tools of research. Would we then say, there exists nothing beyond that which we know? If not, then there should not be any hesitation to believe a thing like soul, which should be of no difficulty for God to create. It should also be true that in the end He will gather us all together. Truth is:

"He whom God guides,
He alone has found the right way,
Whereas for those whom He
lets go astray,
Thou can never find anyone
to protect them besides Him
and We shall gather them together
On the Day of Resurrection,
Prone upon their faces,
blind and dumb and deaf,
with hell as their goal,
Every time the fire abates,
We shall increase for them its blazing flames,
Such will be their equital for having rejected
Our message and having said,
"After we will have become bones, and dust,
Shall we, sure be raised from the
dead in a way of new creation".

٩٧ وَمَن يَهْدِ ٱللَّهُ فَهُوَ ٱلْمُهْتَدِ ۖ وَمَن يُضْلِلْ
فَلَن تَجِدَ لَهُمْ أَوْلِيَآءَ مِن دُونِهِۦ ۖ وَنَحْشُرُهُمْ
يَوْمَ ٱلْقِيَٰمَةِ عَلَىٰ وُجُوهِهِمْ عُمْيًا وَبُكْمًا
وَصُمًّا ۖ مَّأْوَىٰهُمْ جَهَنَّمُ ۖ كُلَّمَا خَبَتْ زِدْنَٰهُمْ
سَعِيرًا

٩٨ ذَٰلِكَ جَزَآؤُهُم بِأَنَّهُمْ كَفَرُوا۟ بِـَٔايَٰتِنَا
وَقَالُوٓا۟ أَءِذَا كُنَّا عِظَٰمًا وَرُفَٰتًا أَءِنَّا
لَمَبْعُوثُونَ خَلْقًا جَدِيدًا

And they are not aware that God,
Who has created the heavens and
earth, has the power to create them
anew in their likeness;
Only He has decreed a term, appointed
for their resurrection, of which there is no doubt,
However all such evildoers are
unwilling to accept anything but blasphemy"
....17(97–99)

٩٩ • أَوَلَمْ يَرَوْا أَنَّ ٱللَّهَ ٱلَّذِى خَلَقَ ٱلسَّمَـٰوَٰتِ
وَٱلْأَرْضَ قَادِرٌ عَلَىٰٓ أَن يَخْلُقَ مِثْلَهُمْ وَجَعَلَ
لَهُمْ أَجَلًا لَّا رَيْبَ فِيهِ فَأَبَى ٱلظَّـٰلِمُونَ إِلَّا
كُفُورًا

Reason of Accountability

Question may be asked why should God be concerned about the actions of mankind? Holy Quran says it is for man's own good only. Otherwise we are of no use to Him 29(6) Good of our soul in this life and the life hereafter lies in the obeyance of the guidance from God. Animals and plants do not have soul but life only and therefore, are not answerable for their actions.

Moreover, mankind has a unique position in the universe also. Everything, without exception is there to serve their cause. If that is so, one must ask what is the purpose of mankind? Reply of the Holy Quran is that man is made to serve His Creator. One way of fulfilling this obligation is to serve the cause of His other creations, in a system; where one is for all, and all are made to serve the one. This is an act of worship, a supreme form of which is to establish peace and harmony in nature. On this, order of God is;

"Don not make mischief in the earth,
After We have set it right"
....

Explaining this an Islamic Saint had said "successful man is that who leaves this world better than he found it". Opposite to it is the guilty soul, that is a mischief oriented soul, which slips down and down in the ranks (السافلين). A noble soul is that which works to establish peace in nature, and thus proves wrong the misgivings of the angels who at the time of the Divine decision of creation of Adam, had expressed the fear,2(30-39) that he will cause mischief in the land. And God had said; "Those who believe

in Me would not do so". These truly are the 'vicegerents of God' on earth, as the revelation says:—

"He it is, Who has made you,
Regents in the earth,
so he who disbeliefs,
his disbelief is on his own
head"
. . . .35(39).

٣٩ هُوَ الَّذِي جَعَلَكُمْ خَلَائِفَ فِي الْأَرْضِ ۚ
فَمَنْ كَفَرَ فَعَلَيْهِ كُفْرُهُ ۖ

"He has made for your control,
all that is in the heavens,
and all that is in the earth.
Behold.
Herein varily are signs
For those who think"
. . . .45(13)

١٣ وَسَخَّرَ لَكُم مَّا فِي السَّمَاوَاتِ وَمَا فِي
الْأَرْضِ جَمِيعًا مِّنْهُ ۚ إِنَّ فِي ذَٰلِكَ لَآيَاتٍ لِّقَوْمٍ
يَتَفَكَّرُونَ

He granteth wisdom
To whom He pleaseth;
And he to whom wisdom
Is granted receiveth
Indeed a benefit overflowing;
But none will grasp the Message
But men of understanding.
2(269)

٢٦٩- يُؤْتِي الْحِكْمَةَ مَن يَشَاءُ ۚ
وَمَن يُؤْتَ الْحِكْمَةَ
فَقَدْ أُوتِيَ خَيْرًا كَثِيرًا ۗ
وَمَا يَذَّكَّرُ إِلَّا أُولُو الْأَلْبَابِ ○

It is clear from these verses that the purpose of universes is to serve the cause of mankind. Therefore purpose of mankind can be nothing else but to serve the cause of the Creator of the universe. A soul develops proportionally to the effort it puts into prove itself worthy of the grand status of being God's vicegerent on the earth. Life of a faithful servant should be for the pleasure of his master. If he ignores, disobeys or rebels then there should be nothing for him but punishment for his ungratefulness.

Resurrection and Accountability

Doomsday is a step towards the universal Day of Accountability for the mankind from everywhere who had been ever there in the domain of time and space.Concept of Accountability is thus connected with the Doomsday and Resurrection;the formerbeing the period of change over,the latter being the 'Day of judgement' This is one of the fundamental articles of faith in the religion of Islam and has been assured in the Holy Quran again and again.

Sometimes account of the Doomsday and Resurrection is given separately but on many occasions it goes together in the same verse. Following are some of the verses highlighting these epoch events of human history of future;

"Warn them (O,Prophet of God),
of the Day of approaching (Doom)"
. . . 40(18)

وَأَنذِرْهُمْ يَوْمَ الْآزِفَةِ ⑱

"It is but one shout,
And behold,
All of them will be brought
before Us"
. . . 36(53)

إِن كَانَتْ إِلَّا صَيْحَةً وَاحِدَةً فَإِذَا هُمْ جَمِيعٌ
لَّدَيْنَا مُحْضَرُونَ ⑮

أَلَا يَظُنُّ أُولَٰئِكَ أَنَّهُم مَّبْعُوثُونَ ④

"Do they not think,
That they will be called to account,
On a Very Big Day"
. . . .83(4,5).

لِيَوْمٍ عَظِيمٍ ⑤

In the verse 83(5) Divine use of the term "Very Big Day" (ليوم عظيم) obviously means that period of the change-over of the present order into the new order is going to be of cosmological duration. It could last for millions of years, may even be longer than the total existence of the present order of the universe. May be less. Knowledge is with God only. After the Doomsday there would be the Day of Accountability. Following verses specifically describe that grand event:

"Then there comes,
The great overwhelming Event,
The Day when Mankind
shall remember,
what they strived for?
. . . .79(34–35)

فَإِذَا جَاءَتِ الطَّامَّةُ الْكُبْرَىٰ ㉞

يَوْمَ يَتَذَكَّرُ الْإِنسَانُ مَا سَعَىٰ ㉟

"No soul will have power,
On any other soul on that Day,
The absolute command is of Allah's only"
. . . .82(19)

يَوْمَ لَا تَمْلِكُ نَفْسٌ لِّنَفْسٍ شَيْئًا
وَالْأَمْرُ يَوْمَئِذٍ لِّلَّهِ ⑲

Resurrection is the Day of justice for all mankind, of all the worlds, of all the times. Earth is just one of those multitude of worlds. How shall it happen, this is a Divine secret, of which our knowledge is extremely limited. However, as we see from the verses 19(94-95) even that should be according to some Divine System of Calculations:

"He takes an account of them (all)
And has numbered them exactly,
And every one of them,
will come to Him singly,
On the Day of Judgement"
....19(94-95).

(94) لَقَدْ أَحْصَاهُمْ وَعَدَّهُمْ عَدًّا
(95) وَكُلُّهُمْ آتِيهِ يَوْمَ الْقِيَامَةِ فَرْدًا

Believe or not Believe.

There are still many people who find it difficult to believe in all this. For them, this life is the only life and there is nothing after death. Ironically, beholders of such beliefs try to justify this on the basis of common sense and science. Not only that, they consider themselves more progressive and forward looking but also to those who do not share their views they give them names such as old fashioned, traditionalists and backward looking people. Oddly enough, they never realize that disbelief is as old-fashioned as the belief itself. Even at the time when the Holy Quran was being revealed, there were people who did not believe in the life after death. Their arguments were almost the same as those of the so call progressive minds of today. Holy Quran says:–

"The chiefs of the people do not
believe and deny the life to come .. 23(23)
They say,
There is no other life but this world's
We die and we live
And there is no rising for us
from the dead" 23(37)

(33) وَقَالَ الْمَلَأُ مِنْ قَوْمِهِ الَّذِينَ
كَفَرُوا وَكَذَّبُوا بِلِقَاءِ الْآخِرَةِ
(37) إِنْ هِيَ إِلَّا حَيَاتُنَا الدُّنْيَا
نَمُوتُ وَنَحْيَا وَمَا نَحْنُ بِمَبْعُوثِينَ

Thus disbelief in the life-after-death has been generally fashionable with the rich exploiting classes of the society. They neither fear Allah by themselves, nor they like the others to be guided on the right path. Without any proof they insist upon their ignorance and wish others to follow them in darkness. On the other hand, a believer has much more solid arguments to believe that death is not the end of the story of life. Even the simple law of cause and effect tells him that there can never be the 'absolute end' of any thing. How can that be with the universe, or with the man, the supreme of creations in the universe? What we call life-after-death is infact the continuation of the present order of existence, where the old memories survive. It is a world as a consequence of the present world. Existence must continue for ever, though its shape and style may vary over time and space. Accordingly, the existence of the pre-universe was also not the "Nothingness"[28] And even if we call it 'Nothingness', it was not devoid of existence. The energy beings, such as Jinns, and angels, had lived even before our material universe. Soul of the man, similarly, would live on after this universe. And there has to be a Day of Judgement, when Justice is done with everyone, rich and the poor, powerful and the weak, intelligent and the fool, good and the bad, alike. That would be the Resurrection, when death will be put to death for ever. We come from Allah and shall go back to Allah. Therefore see that we do not meet Him in a state that we are ashamed of ourselves. Is it not time for review?

Prophet of Allah said,

"Establish your contact with God, through His constant rememberance" (Ibne-Maja).

Fig.27. Arrow diagram of the influences on life and the Resultant Transformation.

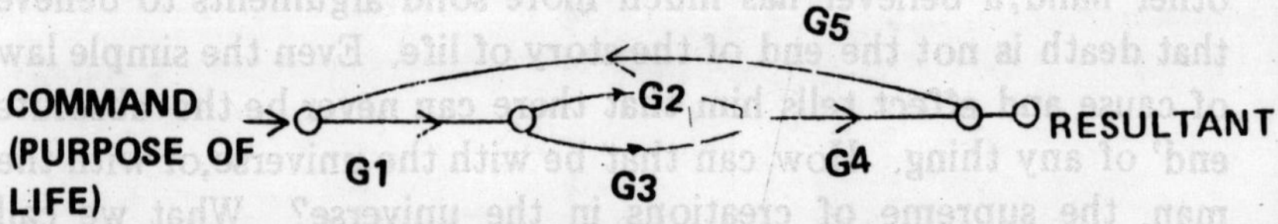

G1= GUIDANCE FROM WITHIN THE GENES PRE-PROGRAMMED.

G2= ACQUIRED GUIDANCE FROM SOCIETY

G3= ACQUIRED GUIDANCE FROM REVELATIN

G4= ASSUMED GUIDANCE WITH CHOICE

G5= REVIEW FOR THE DESIRED RESULTS

Man's life is a feed back system, influenced by his internal genetic code and outside social, religions, educational impacts etc. His personality is the resultant of all such influences. All this may be analysed through the feed back control system theory. The successful life is that which has a soul in peace with his Creator. All is well that ends well.

THE SOUL AND HIM WHO PERFECTED IT. AND INSPIRED IT WITH (CONSCIOUSNESS)

WHAT IS GOOD FOR IT AND WHAT IS WRONG FOR IT AND HE IS INDEED SUCCESSFUL WHO CAUSES IT TO GROW AND HE IS A FAILURE WHO STUNTS IT...
.... 91(7-10)

٧- وَنَفْسٍ وَّمَا سَوّٰىهَا ۝

٨- فَأَلْهَمَهَا فُجُورَهَا وَتَقْوٰىهَا ۝

٩- قَدْ أَفْلَحَ مَنْ زَكّٰىهَا ۝

١٠- وَقَدْ خَابَ مَنْ دَسّٰىهَا ۝

Chapter-22

LIFE IN THE OTHER WORLDS

Is there life anywhere, up there? This is a subject of interest to human beings since long and many best-seller science fictions have been written on this idea. Recently this subject has acquired serious scientific interest also. At first, the planet Mars was considered a popular candidate for life. But space probes have ruled out the possibility, even of the elementary type of life anywhere in our solar system. Except the Earth, all the rest of the solar system is now supposed to be lifeless, dead and barren. However for the universe, scientists believe that intelligent living-beings must be present[11] not at one place but in millions of places in the countless solar systems in the heavenly worlds around us.

It should not be a surprise that on this subject scientific thinking is very much in line with the Holy Quran, which being a revelation from the Creator of the universe, fourteen hundred years ago, had informed that life is not the sole possession of the Earth. Allah is not the Lord of this world but He is the Lord of all the worlds in the universe (رب العالمين). Concept of plurality of the living worlds was in fact introduced at the very outset of the Holy Quran when it said;

"All praise is for Allah,
The Sustainer and Nourisher
of the Worlds,
The Beneficent, The Merciful"
....1(i-2)

الْحَمْدُ لِلَّهِ رَبِّ الْعَالَمِينَ ②

الرَّحْمَٰنِ الرَّحِيمِ ③

Thus at its very opening, Holy Quran broke the age-old-idea of the uniqueness of the Earthly world and introduced the concept of the cosmic unity. The same fact was described even more explicitly in the verse 45(37) which says:—

"All praise be to Allah,
Sustainer and Nourisher
of the heavens,
Sustainer and Nourisher
of the earth, and
Sustainer and Nourishers
of the Worlds"
....45(37)

٣٦ فَلِلَّهِ الْحَمْدُ رَبِّ السَّمٰوٰتِ وَرَبِّ الْأَرْضِ رَبِّ
الْعٰلَمِينَ

From this verse we find that the whole scenario of existence has been classified into three categories i.e. heavens; earth, and other worlds. It is obvious, that all these must have living beings which need nourishments and God arranges and provides for them. Therefore as for life is concerned, our earth cannot be unique in the universe. Contrary to that there should be many more worlds besides it which have the beings like us and God looks after them and meets their demands as He does for us.

As for the nature of these worlds, from the verse 65(12) we see that they are similar to our Earth;

"Allah it is, Who has created,
seven heavens,
and of the earth like thereof..
The commandment comes down
among them gradually,
so that ye may know that
Allah is able to do all things,
He surrounds all things in knowledge"
....65(12)

١٢ اللَّهُ الَّذِي خَلَقَ سَبْعَ سَمٰوٰتٍ وَمِنَ
الْأَرْضِ مِثْلَهُنَّ يَتَنَزَّلُ الْأَمْرُ بَيْنَهُنَّ
لِتَعْلَمُوا أَنَّ اللَّهَ عَلَىٰ كُلِّ شَيْءٍ قَدِيرٌ وَأَنَّ اللَّهَ
قَدْ أَحَاطَ بِكُلِّ شَيْءٍ عِلْمًا

With reference to the plurality of heavens, this revelation clearly speaks about the plurality of the earth-like-heavenly bodies. In his interpretation of this verse, Maulana-Abu-Al-Ala Moudoodi[8] says that Ibn-e-Abbas, a great scholar of Holy Quran and a direct disciple of the Prophet of Allah (peace be upon him), in the first century of Hijra, believed with confidence that there are many more earth like bodies in the heavens. However, he would not say it o p e n l y fearing t h a t people may get confused. He thought that not only those earths are inhabited by the intelligent beings but also their people are exactly like the mankind on earth. They have a Prophet like Muhammad (peace be upon him), and have Adam, like our Adam, a Noah, like our Noah, an Ibrahim like our Ibrahim, and Jesus like our Jesus, (peace be upon them). Thus according to Abdullah bin Abbas, creation pattern is similar to the earth, any where else in the universe also.

Probably Abdullah bin-Abbas had derived his idea of human beings living in other places of universe, from the prophet of Allah when he said, "When you sit down in the prayer for Attahayat (التحيات) and say: "peace be upon us, and the righteous people of God" (السلام علينا وعلى عباد الله الصالحين) you actually send peace on every righteous servant of God living on earth and in the heavens". This clearly implied that good and bad, all type of people also live in the other places in cosmos besides our earth.

Like the earth, presence of intelligent-living-beings in the outer space is also confirmed from the verse 55(29), which says:

"Of Him seeks (its needs)
Every one in the heavens and earth;
And on the earth,
Everyday, He appears in
New splendour"
... 55(29)

٢٩ يَسْـَٔلُهُۥ مَن فِى ٱلسَّمَٰوَٰتِ وَٱلْأَرْضِ ۚ كُلَّ يَوْمٍ هُوَ فِى شَأْنٍ

Another direct reference to the life in other heavenly systems is found in the verse ***42(29)*** also, which says;

"Among His signs, is the creation
of heavens and the earth,
And the living creatures
He has dispersed therein,
And He is able to gather them together
when He wills"
... 42(29)

٢٩ وَمِنْ ءَايَٰتِهِۦ خَلْقُ ٱلسَّمَٰوَٰتِ وَٱلْأَرْضِ وَمَا بَثَّ فِيهِمَا مِن دَآبَّةٍ ۚ وَهُوَ عَلَىٰ جَمْعِهِمْ إِذَا يَشَآءُ قَدِيرٌ

It is obvious from this verse that living creatures, as on earth, must be widely scattered among the heavenly worlds also.

It also means that cosmos has innumerous living worlds

with all type of animals, beasts and human beings dispersed there-in. Moreover, new worlds are constantly being added to the universe, befitting for carrying life. At their turn, each one of them would have also its own Doomsday.

In the verse 65(12), the statement that 'Commandant comes down among them gradually' (يتنزل الأمر) is also of great significance, this means that development of each one of these earth systems is a slow evolutionary process. Turbulence is basically a feature of the hot and active systems such as Nebulae etc., but once a heavenly body is destined to become a life supporting place, the process of change is slowed down there 28

An example of this slow change is our own earth. According to the current scientific thought, it is about 4 to 5 billions years old and has slowly evolved to its present state. First signs of life had appeared on it after several billion years of its existence. Even after that, it took hundreds of millions of years to have mature life on it.

The reason given for slow evolutionary development in the verse 65(12) is that mankind may know thereby, that Allah is able to do all things. This may also mean that one day mankind on earth would come to know of other similar worlds in space. In this process they will also understand the working of their Creator more clearly.

The concept that other earths are like our earth, implies that their development in space may be guided by the similar set of rules, and life pattern in them should be exactly like ours. This must be so because, God who is the Maker of scientific laws is the same everywhere.

Multiplicity of the living worlds would also be the part of the new universe to come after the ultimate doomsday of the present universe. One of these worlds called Janna (جنت), the Hereafter abode of the righteous ones,is described in detail in the Holy Quran. In similitude, some features of this world can be seen in the following verse:—

"A similitude of the Janna, which is promised unto those who keep their duty is that; Underneath it, rivers flow, its food is everlasting, and its shade (also)"
....13(35)

٣٥ * مَثَلُ الْجَنَّةِ الَّتِي وُعِدَ الْمُتَّقُونَ ۖ تَجْرِي مِن تَحْتِهَا الْأَنْهَارُ ۖ أُكُلُهَا دَائِمٌ وَظِلُّهَا

As for the inhabitants of that place, Quran tells:—

"They will say,
praise be to Allah,
Who has truly fulfilled
His promise to us,
And has given us the land in heritage,
We can dwell in the Janna as we will,
How excellent a reward for those.
Who work righteously"

QURAN IN THE OTHER WORLDS

As for the social life of the inhabitants of other worlds, as we could see from the explanation of Ibn-e-Abbas also; they have also their own Holy Books and religions. They all come from the same "Supreme Source of revelation; from which Holy Quran has orginated for us on earth. This also we can see from the following revelation:

"By the Book which makes things clear,
We, have made it a Reading (Quran)
in Arabic,
that ye may be able to understand,
And verily, it is in the 'Mother of the Books
In our presence, high, full of wisdom"
. . . . . 43(2-4).

وَالْكِتٰبِ الْمُبِيْنِ ٢
إِنَّا جَعَلْنٰهُ قُرْءٰنًا عَرَبِيًّا لَّعَلَّكُمْ تَعْقِلُوْنَ ٣
وَإِنَّهٗ فِيْٓ أُمِّ الْكِتٰبِ لَدَيْنَا لَعَلِيٌّ حَكِيْمٌ ٤

This means that Holy Quran is derived from the Mother of the Book (أمّ الكتاب), the supreme moral principle of nature, preserved with the God of universe. The verse 56(75-80)& 85(21-22) refer to this source of wisdom as the "Book well guarded", a tablet preserved".

"This is indeed a Quran, most honourable,
(Preserved) in "The Book well-guarded",
which none shall touch but those,
Who are purified and clean,
A revelation from the Lord
of the Worlds"
... 56(77-80)

إِنَّهٗ لَقُرْءَانٌ كَرِيْمٌ ٧٧
فِيْ كِتٰبٍ مَّكْنُوْنٍ ٧٨
لَّا يَمَسُّهٗٓ إِلَّا الْمُطَهَّرُوْنَ ٧٩
تَنْزِيْلٌ مِّنْ رَّبِّ الْعٰلَمِيْنَ ٨٠

"Nay this is a Glorious Quran,
Inscribed in a Tablet preserved"
. . . 85(21-22)

٢١ بَلْ هُوَ قُرْءَانٌ مَّجِيدٌ
٢٢ فِي لَوْحٍ مَّحْفُوظٍ

Quran (قران) is thus the generic name, a characteristic of the class of God's revelation; a Reading designed for the moral and spiritual development of mankind throughout the universe. And since mankind is the same everywhere, Quran would be the same every where. The verse 81(27) throws light on this concept in the following manner;

"Verily this (Quran) is no less
than a Message,
To (all) the Worlds, Whoever
among you wills to go straight.
But ye shall not,
Except as Allah wills,
The Cherisher of the worlds"
. . .81(27-29)

٢٧ إِنْ هُوَ إِلَّا ذِكْرٌ لِّلْعَالَمِينَ
٢٨ لِمَن شَاءَ مِنكُمْ أَن يَسْتَقِيمَ
٢٩ وَمَا تَشَاءُونَ إِلَّا أَن يَشَاءَ اللَّهُ رَبُّ الْعَالَمِينَ

This proves that Holy Quran, which literally means "Reading" is actually the Divine Book of Cosmic Moral Order, a universal code of guidance for intelligent beings wherever they may be. This explains also the secret of the unique style of this book which is very much different from any other religious or non-religious book. It has an absoluteness and purity of style and theme; which takes it above the bounds of relativity of time and space, rendering it a suitable reading for all the people, of all the times, and of all the worlds. Unlike any other book, read it and re-read for hundred of times, never does it arouse in the faithful any wearingness.[39] In fact through repetition everytime it is still more attractive fresh and loving.

SOCIAL LIFE IN OTHER WORLDS

The evidence of the presence of living beings in the outer space and their social life can also be seen from the dialogue which had taken place between the angels and God at the time of the decision of the creation of the "First Human Being" on the Earth, which is;

"Behold! when thy Lord said to the angels,
I will create a vicegerent on Earth,
(at this) the angels said,
Will Thou place therein, the one
Who will make mischief therein,
and shed blood"
. . .2(30)

٣٠ وَإِذْ قَالَ رَبُّكَ لِلْمَلَٰٓئِكَةِ إِنِّي جَاعِلٌ فِي
الْأَرْضِ خَلِيفَةً قَالُوٓا أَتَجْعَلُ فِيهَا مَن يُفْسِدُ فِيهَا
وَيَسْفِكُ الدِّمَآءَ

This bold assertion of angels about the man yet to be created, could not be without their previous observation of the behaviour of earlier human species because they could not have ventured to predict something without knowledge. Thus creation of man on earth was not the first experiment of its kind in the universe. Angels might had seen some type of homo-Sapiens elsewhere which were mischievous creations making wars and shedding blood of each other. Though man is the superior experiment in creation, yet, when he falls below his status, he is not then above the animals who lived on this earth earlier to him. Men on other places in the cosmos cannot be different from us, since God's pattern of creation remains the same everywhere.[40] Their psychological and physical behaviour pattern should be like ours. Like us they would be having their peace, disputes, battles, wars and peace again. Like ours, their worlds are also perishable and with reference to the verses 55(29-40) one can say that Day of Judgement is also a continuous process on them. It is always happenings on one or the other planets inhabited by mankind in the cosmos. All of them have their accountability at their turns.

MEETING WITH LIVING BEINGS OF OTHER WORLDS

Fourteen hundred years ago, the Holy Quran also pointed out that time would come when the living creatures in the various parts of universe will come closer together, possibly through actual contact or by inter-galactic communication, physically or spirtually. The following revelation is a great promise and

hope for those who are looking for the living beings in the outer space:—

"And among His signs,
is the creation of the heavens and the earth
And the living creatures,
That He has scattered through out them,
And He has the power to gather them together,
when He wills"
...42(29)

٢٩ وَمِنْ ءَايَـٰتِهِۦ خَلْقُ ٱلسَّمَـٰوَٰتِ وَٱلْأَرْضِ
وَمَا بَثَّ فِيهِمَا مِن دَآبَّةٍ ۚ وَهُوَ عَلَىٰ جَمْعِهِمْ
إِذَا يَشَآءُ قَدِيرٌ

Let us hope that in this life or in the life after death, we shall communicate with other beings like us, in the cosmos.

LIFE IN THE INTERPLANETORY SPACES

We have seen from the verses of the Holy Quran quoted herein that life in the heavens is a widespread phenomenon and intelligent living-beings should be present at numerous places in the universe. Most likely life-bearing heavenly bodies are the earth-like-planets of the solar systems. However more striking discovery is that life also exists in the space between the planets and stars, though science generally regards it as the lifeless vacuum only.

So far it has been known that inter-planetory space is litered with stellar gases, sub-atomic particles and some type of subtle matter.[29] This seems to be the first step towards the acknowledgement of the truth expressed in the Holy Quran that creations of God are present everywhere, a fact seen from the following revelations also.

"He is the Nourisher
and Sustainer of all things,
In the heavens and the earth,
and all that is in between them,
The Beneficent, with Whom,
none can converse" **78(37)**

٣٧ رَّبِّ ٱلسَّمَـٰوَٰتِ وَٱلْأَرْضِ وَمَا بَيْنَهُمَا ٱلرَّحْمَـٰنِ
لَا يَمْلِكُونَ مِنْهُ خِطَابًا

"Unto Him belongs,
Whatsoever is in the heavens,
Whatsoever is in the earth,
and whatsoever is in between them
and whatsoever is beneath the soil"
. . .20(6).

٦ لَهُۥ مَا فِى ٱلسَّمَٰوَٰتِ وَمَا فِى ٱلْأَرْضِ
وَمَا بَيْنَهُمَا وَمَا تَحْتَ ٱلثَّرَىٰ

Here are mentioned four categories of things:

Those living in the heavenly bodies,
Those living in the earth;
Those living in the space in between the heavenly bodies
and those living in the depths of the body of the earth.

All these things are in the need of nourishment and maintenance by God, which shows that such things also grow and multiply. As far as the concept of nourishment of things on earth, it is well understood; but we little know the things existing in between the heavenly spaces, in the heavens and beneath the surface of earth and the way they are being nourished. One may suppose that type of interspace things may be some kind of bacterial life, which still remains undiscovered. If that is so, then, here is a point of great caution also; particularly in the field of space research and exploration, because if such living organisms are carried back to earth by the space vehicles, there is the obvious danger of polluting our environment with the unknowns. According to some recent scientific views[11] on the life in the universe, space is seeded with micro-organism in the form of spores. They travel into steller world, puffed by radiation pressure, and can survive the cold and vacuum of space indefinitely. Hoyle and Wikeramsinghe[11] think that life is created in the centre of comets which are gently heated by chemical reactions to temperature above the melting point of water. They further argue that viruses such as influenza may reach the Earth from comets. Whatever the truth, the fact remains that Allah is the Sustainer and Nourisher of all life, the same God every-where, the Maker of the Time and Space.

"And He it is,
Who in the heaven is God,
And in the earth is God,
He is the Wise, the Knower,
Blessed is He,
Unto Whom belongs, the sovereignity
of heavens and the earth,
And all that is in between them,
And with Him is the knowledge of the Hour
(of Doomsday);
Unto Him ye will be returned"
. . . 43(84-85).

٨٤ وَهُوَ ٱلَّذِى فِى ٱلسَّمَآءِ إِلَٰهٌ وَفِى ٱلْأَرْضِ إِلَٰهٌ ۚ
وَهُوَ ٱلْحَكِيمُ ٱلْعَلِيمُ
٨٥ وَتَبَارَكَ ٱلَّذِى لَهُۥ مُلْكُ ٱلسَّمَٰوَٰتِ وَٱلْأَرْضِ
وَمَا بَيْنَهُمَا وَعِندَهُۥ عِلْمُ ٱلسَّاعَةِ وَإِلَيْهِ
تُرْجَعُونَ

Part—IV

Index of the selected Ayats of Holy Quran, about the Doomsdays, Resurrection and the Life after death.

AN INDEX OF THE VERSES OF HOLY QURAN ON THE SUBJECT OF DOOMSDAY

S.No.	Subject	Ayats
		I. Nature
1.	Doomsday is must	4(87),6(135),15(85),18(21),18(98 22(7), 29(5), 30(43), 34(3),40 (59), 42(18, 42(47), 45(26), 45(32), 51(5), 31(6), 51(8-12),52(7-8), 54(46), 56(1-2), 59(15), 70(1-3),77(7) 56(95), 84(6).
2.	Sudden coming of the Doomsday	6(31), 7(187), 12(107), 22(55), 43(66), 47(18), 21(40), 10(45).
3.	It is a secret.	20(15), 7(187), 31(34), 33(63), 43(85), 53(58), 67(26), 79(42).
4.	It is a great event, highly destructive.	38(67-68), 54(46).
5.	It is to come on its own time, a fixed time.	34(30), 78(17), 44(40), 54(46), 78(17), 11(104), 77(12-13).
6.	It is near (relatively) Signs of the Doomsday are already there.	21(1), 21(97), 33(63), 42(17), 53(57-58), 54(1), 70(6-7), 47(18).
		II. Purpose
7.	It is a step toward meeting God.	32(23).
8.	They are doomed who reject it.	77(15), 77(19,24,28,34,37,40,45,49) 83(10-12), 107(1).
9.	Full justice, Reward and Punishment is must.	13(40), 51(6), 78(39),88(26).

10.	**It is a pre-requisite for resurrection.**	**58(6), 64(7), 17(51).**
11.	**All people of all the worlds will be gathered on Resurrection.**	**2(148), 2(203), 3(9,25,158)), 4(87, 172), 5(96),109), 6(12), 6(29), 6(51, 62,72,128), 7(57), 8(24), 9(24), 10(4, 28), 45(26),11(7;18, 103), 14(21),15 (25,36), 17(49,50,51,98,99), 18(47,99), 19(85), 20(55), 23(79,82,100,115), 24 (64), 25(17), 26(87), 29(57), 30(11), 34(26,40), 36(32), 36(53), 37(16,17), 40(16), 42(15), 43(85), 44(40), 45(26, 27), 50(44), 51(42,43), 53(42), 56(47-50), 58(9), 64(9), 67(15-24), 75(12), 77(38), 79(23), 80(22), 83(4-5).**
12.	**Day of Judgement will be over in a short time.**	**16(77), 31(28), 54(50).**

III. Objections of Non Believers about Resurrection

13.	**They say, this life is the only life.**	**6(29), 23(37),44(34-35), 45(24).**
14.	**They say, resurrection is the only the mythology of olden people.**	**13(5), 17(49-98), 23(35-36.82-83), 27((67-68), 32(10), 36(78), 37(16-17, 53), 75(3,4,5,6), 79(10-11), 82(9).**
15.	**They say, life after death is simply a belief of wich-crafts.**	**11(7)**
16.	**They doubt meeting with God.**	**22(5), 41(54).**
17.	**They say, resurrection is an illogical thing.**	**50(3).**
18.	**They bet that life after death is not possible.**	**16(38-39).**

IV. Great Events of the Earthly Doomsday

19.	Soor a trumpet like sound which will make people unconscious, and later raise them again.	18(49), 20(102), 23(101), 27(87), 30(25), 36(51-53), 38(15), 39(68), 50(20), 50(42), 69(13), 74(8), 78(18), 79(13-14).
20.	An animal will emerge from ground which will speak with people.	27(82).
21.	Earth will burst.	36(51-53), 50(44), 54(7), 70(43), 79(13-14), 82(4), 99(6), 100(9).
22.	Mountain will fly like carded wool.	18(47), 20(105-107), 27(88), 52(10), 56(5-6), 69(14-15), 70(9), 72(10),73 (14), 77(10), 78(20), 81(3), 101(5).
23.	Continuous earthquakes.	22(1), 56(4), 73(14), 79(6-7),99(1).
24.	Sunlight will be folded up.	81(1).
25.	Earth will be pounded over pounded.	56(4), 69(14), 89(21).
26.	Earth crust will burst upside down.	84(4),5), 99(2,3).
27.	Earth will tell its tales secret will be out.	99(4,5), 86(9), 100(10).
28.	Earth will be levelled of.	18(4), 84(3).
29.	Wall of Zulqurnain will fall.	18(98).
30.	Jooj-Majooj will spread over earth.	18(99), 21(96).
31.	Seas will boil over.	81(6), 82(3).
32.	Beasts and pregnant camels will wander around masterless.	81(4), 81(5).

33.	Earth will be reduced barren.	18(8).
34.	Sound of Soor will be heard by everyone as near.	20(108), 36(53), 50(41), 54(6).
35.	Moon will eclipse (for ever).	75(8).
36.	Moon will join sun.	75(9).
37.	Light that will dazzle the eyes.	75(7).
38.	Pregnants loose pregnancy	22(2).
39.	People get unconscious	2(22).
40.	People will scatter like moth.	54(7), 101(4).
41.	Man cannot imagine the destructive nature of the Doomsday.	69(1-3), 77(14), 82(17-18).

V. Event of the Heavenly Doomsday

42.	Doomsdays of worlds other than earth.	55(31).
43.	The heaven will sent asunder.	25(25), 55(37), 69(16), 73(18), 77(9), 78(19), 82(1), 84(1-2).
44.	Stars will loose light and fall off.	77(8), 81(2), 82(2).
45.	Sky barrier will fall apart.	81(11).
46.	Heaven will look like molten copper bath.	70(8), 55(37).
47.	Heaven will shiver.	52(9).
48.	Heaven will bring smoke	44(10), 39(68).

49.	Soor sound will make everyone in the heavens and earth unconscious except that Allah wills.	22(2), 27(87), 39(68), 52(45).

VI. New Universe

50.	Heavens and earth will be rolled together like the scroll of papers.	21(104), 39(67).
51.	In the reconstruction present heavens and earth will be changed into some other form.	14(48).
52.	Ultimately before the resurrection everything will destroy.	55(26).

VII. Resurrection and Justice

53.	Each one will be brought to life again even if one is fossilized as a stone, iron or harder thing.	17(51).
54.	Resurrection is the responsibility of Allah.	53(47).
55.	On the resurrection, people will rise from their graves.	2(28), 2(73,203, 259,260), 6(36), 6(60) 7(14), 7(24), 7(36), 16(21-38), 22(5-7, 66), 23(16), 26(81-87), 27(65), 30(19, 25,40,50,56), 31(28), 36(52-79), 37(144), 38(79), 42(9), 58(6-18), 64(7) 67(15), 71(18), 72(7), 83(4-6), 89 (25), 101(9).

56.	Resurrection is easy for Allah. It is like the first creation. In the Resurrection people will assemble in groups and nations.	64(7), 18(48), 21(104), 30(14), 78(18) 99(6), 45(28), 81(7).
57.	(New) Earth will shine with the nur of its Lord.	39(69).
58.	Each one will have a driver and a witness with him.	4(41), 28(75), 50(21).
59.	People will feel the total life of the world as the duration of an evening or morning.	10(45), 23(112-114), 30(55), 46(35), 79(46).
60.	Those who know, will say it has been a long period.	30(56), 20(104).
61.	There will be two main groups, righteous and the accused ones.	11(105), 30(43).
62.	People will recognize each other.	10(45).
63.	Each one will be concerned about his own fate only and runaway from his relatives.	16(11), 80(37), 80(34-36).
64.	It will be a very difficult day for the rejectors.	25(26), 54(8), 73(17), 74(9-10), 76(10).
65.	Rejectors will be recognized by their foreheads and skins.	55(40-41).
66.	The believers will have no fear.	21(103), 27(89), 43(68-69).
67.	None will bear the burden of others.	6(164), 17(15), 35(18), 39(7), 53(38), 82(19).

68.	No excuse will be accepted.	34(31-33), 38(61), 40(47-50), 50(27-28).
69.	All deeds and thoughts will be presented and accounted for full justice.	21(47), 2(81), 2(110), 7(8-9), 23(102-103), 101(6-11), 3(25), 161, 185)), 7(147), 52(16), 53(41), 76(22).
70.	None will be wronged.	2(272,281), 3(25,161), 4(40,49), 6(160), 10(54),11(109,112)), 16(111), 17(71), 18(49), 19(60), 20(112), 21(47), 23(62), 36(54), 39(69), 40(17), 45(22), 46(19), 52(21).

REFERENCES

1. Fred Hoyle, "Nature of the Universe" Book Pub. Penguin Press, 1964.
2. John Gribbin, "Precise measurements of Bothing Pin Down the Universe" New Scientist, 15 December, 1983.
3. James Gleik, "Galaxies Reported Moving at High Speeds", New York Times, December 2, 1981.
4. Verses 20(6), 45(37), 55(29), 13(35), 78(36-38), Holy Quran.
5. Baker and Fredrick, "An Introduction to Astronomy", Book Pub. Bannostrand Co. Holland.
6. Michael D.Lenonick, "A Wonder in the Southern Sky", Time March 9, 1987.
7. Time, "Did Comments kill the Dinosaures", (Page 45-45), May 6, 1985.
8. Abu-Ala Maududi, "Tafhim-ul-Quran," Vol 5, Pub. Tarjman-ul-Quran, Lahore.
9. Thornton Page and Lou Page, "The Origin of the Solar System", The Macmillan Co. New York-1966.
10. Paul Davies, "God and the New Physics", Book Published by Simson Schuster, Inc. New York, 1983.
11. Robert Hutchison, "The Search for our Beginning", Book pages 150-156, pub. British Museum Natural History, Offord University Press, 1983.
12. Imam Ghazali, "Ahyae-ul-Aloom.
13. I.D.Novikov, "Evolution of the Universe", Cambridge University Press, 1983.
14. Muhammad Asad, "Sahih-Al-Bukhari, translated and explained" page 241, 241 Pub. Dar-Al Andalus Gibralter, 1981.
15. Muhammad Asad, "The Message of the Quran" Translation and Commentry of the Holy Quran, Pub. Dar-Al-Andulus, Gibralter, Pub. 1980.
16. Vincent Gronim, "The view from Planet Earth" (Book published by Collins St. James Place, London. 1980.
17. I.D.Novikov, "Evolution of the Universe", Book English edition Pub. Cambridge University Press, London.
18. Fred Hoyle, "The Nature of the Universe", Book, Pub. Penguin Press, page 64.
19. Maulana Madoodi, "Tafhim-ul-Quran", Commentry on the Holy Quran, Urdu.
20. 13(38-39), 10(3), 30(30), 50(24), 7(83), 68(45),4(6), Holy Quran.
21. W.L.Stokes, "Essentials of Earth History", Book. Pub. Prentice Hall USA.
22. Appendix—I given herewith.
23. Thornton Page, Lou W.Page, "The origin of the Solar System", Book page 308-310.
24. Salim Mahmood, "Modern Developments in Science and Technology", Vol.II Pub. SUPARCO,Karachi, in 1985.
25. Robert Moody, "Life after Death" Book-Published, USA.
26. Ahmad Raza Khan, "The World of Souls (Urdu Book)" 1910, Reprinted by Farid Book Dept. Lahore, 1984.
27. Bill Liller and Ben Mayer, "The Cambridge Astronomy Guide; 1985.
28. Bashiruddin Mahmood, "A new look into the creation and evolution of Universe, as seen through the Holy Quran", Book under print.
29. Michael Zelik, "Astronomy the evolving universe," Fourth Edition, Published by Harper & Row, New York, 1985.
30. Allama Sir MUhammad Iqbal, "The Reconstruction of Religious Thought in Islam", reprinted by Javed Iqbal in 1962, Pub. Sheikh Ashraf Ali, Lahore.
31. James Geik, "Galaxies reported moving at High speed", Science Times, New York Times Dec.2, 1986.
32. Maurice Bucaille, "The Bible, The Quran and Science" English Edition Pub. 1979 by Aisha Bawani Trust, Karachi.
33. W.B.S.Rabbani, "Islamic Sufism" Book Published by Sufi Foundation Lahore, 1984.
34. Sten Odenwald, "To the Big Bang and Beyond", Astronomy, Vol.15, No.5, May, 1987, USA.
35. Bashiruddin Mahmood, "Symmetry of the Universe and Quranic Principle of Pairs", Paper presented at the Second International Conference on Quran and Science, Held on 17th June 1987 at Karachi.

36. Ali Akbar, "Israel and the Prophecies of the Holy Quran" Book Published eighth edition 1977, by Seraj Publication, Leckwith, Cardiff, U.K.
37. Gamow, "The Birth and Death of the Sun",Book, Published by the New American Library, New York.
38. Bashiruddin Mahmood, "Creation and Evolution of Earth as seen through the Holy Quran", Book under preparation.
39. Muhammad Marmaduke Pickthal, "The Glorious Quran", English Translation of the Holy Quran, First published in 1932.
40. Bashiruddin Mahmood, 'Fundamental of Sience in the Holy Quran",Book to be printed, Holy Quran Research Foundation, Islamabad.
41. Ali Al Tantawi, English Translation, Babur Ali Zia, "Fundamentals of Faith in Islam",Pub. Idara-e-Ilmul Quran, Lahore, Pakistan, 1983.
42. Allama Abdullah Yousuf Ali, "The Holy Quran" English translation, pub. by Sh. Muhammad Ashraf, Lahore.
43. Mir Mohammad Hussain, "Mazamin-e-Quran" i.e. Index of the Holy Quran (Urdu) Book published by Islamic Publications, Lahore.
44. Bukhari, Muslim Chapter Alfitna.
45. Dr. Muhammad Mohsin Khan, 'Arabic-English Translation of Sahih Al-Bukhari" Vol.IX Chapter Fitnah-Hadith 234,Pub. Kazi Publications, Lahore.
46. Prof. Abdus Salam, 'The symmetry concepts in modern physics", Pub. Atomic Energy Centre, Lahore, 1966.

INTRODUCTION
TO
HOLY QURAN RESEARCH FOUNDATION

AIM:

"And indeed We have displayed for mankind,
In this Quran all kind of simlitudes,
But most of them refuse, aught save disbelief"
. . . . .17(89)

The Holy Quran Research Foundation established in November, 1986, is a volunteer body set up with the aim to carrying out in-depth study of the Holy Quran; and with its reference conduct research into scientific and social subjects of importance to our age and society.

It is based upon the conviction that Holy Quran is the Word of Allah, available to us in the purest form, exactly as it was revealed to the last of His prophets, Muhammad, may peace and blessing of Allah be upon him. As such it needs no proof for its verocity and if any branch of the existing body of human knowledge, science or philosophy does not fit well into it or fall short of it, then it is the latter which needs a review and be corrected. The Foundation is thus dedicated to the dissemination of the Message of Allah and promotion of human knowledge based upon Holy Quran and the Sunnah of the Prophet of Allah.

MODE OF OPERATION:

The Foundation achieves its objectives by identifying a broad range of topics and extending an open invitation to students of the Holy Quran from all walks of life to carryout research into them. Invitation to carry out research is not limited to the religious scholars alone but is extended to all persons who may otherwise be engaged in any material profession but are keen to disseminate the message of the Holy Quran.

The Foundation and its associated bodies then select suitable number of scholars to carry out research on assigned topics, provide an institutional framework to the scholars; assist and coordinate their research work, hold periodic discussion groups, brain storming sessions, seminars; and review meetings; and on approval by a pannel of experts, undertake the publication and distribution of the research works on world-wide basis.

ACCOUNTS:

All accounts of the Foundation are auditable which it maintains in the name of "*Holy Quran Research Foundation, National Bank of Pakistan, F-7/2 Branch*, Islamabad". Sources of funds are the volunteer contributions, proceeds from the sale of its books and membership fees.

GOVERNING BODY

All affairs of the Foundation are decided mutually by a Governing Body, consisting of ten executive members, including the Chairman, Treasurer, Secretary and Joint Secretary, as per the approved rules and By-Laws of the Foundation.

MEMBERSHIP

Membership of the Foundation is open to all muslims of the world who share the objectives of the Foundation and wish to work for the pleasure of Allah and His Rasool (S.A.W) for the dissemination of the knowledge about the Holy Quran and the Sunnah of the prophet of Allah on world-wide basis; And who firmly believe that the process of Divine revelation was completed on the Holy Prophet and Holy Quran is the last of the revealed books, which confirms and completes the Truth of all the earlier prophets, may peace be upon them. As such there remains neither the need, nor will he born any other prophet after him, and if anyone claims or has claimed to be prophet, he is/was a liar.

PRIVILEGES OF THE MEMBERS

All members are kept posted of the activities of the Foundation and provided with the library facilities, research papers and scholarly work about the Holy Quran on regular basis. They are also provided with the institutional framework for the deeper study of the Holy Quran and the Sunnah of the Prophet of Allah; and encouraged to write their findings and publish them on world-wide basis after review and approval by the Foundation.

MEMBERSHIP FEE

Membership fee is on annual basis through cheque in the name of the Holy Quran Research Foundation, Islamabad according to the following rates:—

For Pakistan:	Rs.100/- per annum
For other countries:	U.S.$25/- or equivalent currency per annum.

October 1st, 1987
Islamabad.

S.Bashiruddin Mahmood
(Founder) Chairman,
Holy Quran Research Foundation.